ENGLISH ✛ HERITAGE

Book of
Life in Roman Britain

For Professor Emerita Rosalind M.T. Hill,
who set me on the historical path
and guided my steps thereafter,
in affectionate gratitude.

ENGLISH ✜ HERITAGE

Book of
Life in
Roman Britain

Joan P. Alcock

B. T. Batsford / English Heritage
London

First published 1996
Reprinted 2000

Typeset by Bernard Cavender Design & Greenwood Graphics Publishing
Printed and bound in Great Britain by Redwood Books, Trowbridge, Wiltshire

Published by B.T. Batsford Ltd
9 Blenheim Court, Brewery Road, London N7 9NT

A member of the Chrysalis Group plc

A CIP catalogue record for this book is
available from the British Library

ISBN 0 7134 6364 3 (cased)
0 7134 6745 2 (limp)

(*Front cover*) The Ermine Street Guard on parade in London
(*photograph © Museum of London/Ermine Street Guard*).

Contents

Illustrations

Colour plates

Acknowledgements

The origins of this book lay in an invitation by Peter Kemmis Betty to revise Antony Birley's *Life in Roman Britain*, published by Batsford in 1964. This covered the whole spectrum of Roman Britain but so much had been discovered in the last thirty years that a revision proved impossible. The present volume is more selective, considering civilian rather than army life, and social aspects rather than military or political. In some cases the evidence allows firm statements to be made; in others, there can only be speculative views, which change as further evidence comes to light. I have based my conclusions on both of these concepts.

I am most grateful to a number of persons, organizations and museums, to which copyright belongs, for permission to reproduce the following photographs and drawings: The Trustees of the British Museum (**2, 6, 8, 58, 64**), The

Grosvenor Museum, Chester (**63**), The Corinium Museum, Cirencester (**47**), Colchester Museums (**42**), the City Museum and Art Gallery, Gloucester (**65**), The Leeds Museums and Galleries, City Museum (**76**), Rijksmuseum van Oudheden, Leiden, Holland (**48**), Lincolnshire County Council, City and County Museum (**44**), The Museum of London (**26**), Crown Copyright: Royal Commission on the Historical Monuments of England (**19, 25, 27, 29, 30, 34, 37, 43, 45, 59, 60-2, 70, 77**), The Trustees of the National Museums of Scotland (**22, 56**), St Albans Museums (**13, 39**), Tyne and Wear Museums (**4**), The National Museums and Galleries of Wales (**40**), The Warburg Institute (**18, 35, 49, 54**). The copyright for **9-11, 15-17, 20, 23, 31, 41, 46, 52, 57, 66, 69, 72, 75, 78, 79, colour plates 1, 2, 4-7, 9, 11-13** belongs to English Heritage.

The quotation from *A Shropshire Lad* by A. E. Housman is reproduced by permission of The Society of Authors as the literary representative of the Estates of A. E. Housman. Peter Connolly very kindly gave permission for me to reproduce his illustration of the Housesteads latrine (**colour plate 10**). Mark Sorrell gave permission to reproduce the drawing by Alan Sorrell of the Bath temple–theatre complex (**73**). Judith Dobie of English Heritage provided illustrations (**10, 11, 31, 52, 66, 72** and **colour plate 7**) which re-create the life-style as it might have been in Roman Britain and I am grateful to her and to my colleagues Anne-Marie Scott (**12, 24, 28, 36**) and Hilary Dalke (**5, 7, 33, 55, 67, 68**) of the South Bank University, London, for their drawings. Photographs (**3, 14, 21, 32, 50, 51, 53, 71, 80, 81; colour plates 3, 8**) and one drawing (**74**) are provided by the author.

Andrew Costin of the National Bakery School, South Bank University, experimented over several days to produce Roman-style bread baked in the shape and style of loaves found at Pompeii (**53 and colour plate 8**). The result was both convincing in shape and edible in consumption.

Encouragement to write and rewrite the text was provided by a number of friends and I am most grateful to Phyllis Kern for meticulously checking the text and to Margaret Roxan of the Institute of Archaeology, University of London, for her help in discussing problems relating to the history of Roman Britain. Jennifer Harris of RCHME, Lucy Bunning of English Heritage and Clare Sunderland of Batsford helped my search for photographs in their organizations.

Peter Kemmis Betty and Stephen Johnson gave constructive advice to help to reduce the text to reasonable and readable length. Finally my thanks must go to Charlotte Vickerstaff whose help was invaluable.

Introduction

Empathy, currently in vogue at the moment, is to identify with the life of a person living in another era. To some extent, this identification may be achieved. A person wearing a toga realizes a dignified effort has to be made when walking in such a garment. Experiments in grinding corn, making bread with the resulting flour, boiling joints in a pit of water heated by pot-boilers, can give an indication of food habits. But anyone living in this century cannot hope to emulate a Roman lifestyle. When a group of people attempted to live for several months under conditions devised to be akin to those in the Iron Age, the experiment terminated in disagreement and revolt against their miserable conditions. Possibly the main problem was that a natural leader imbued with authority never emerged; such a leader would have been to the forefront in the Iron Age. The advantages of civilization are seductive. Tacitus, writing at the end of the first century AD, mentioned 'porticoes, baths and sumptuous banquets' as amenities which the Britons found agreeable; our era might add the blessings of sanitation, the freezer and the microwave.

This is not to say that some insight cannot be gained into the lives of people who once lived in Roman Britain. The evidence includes the sites themselves. Standing beneath the walls of Richborough, Kent, or gazing down from the later Norman tower at the Saxon Shore fort of Portchester in Hampshire reveals the strength of forts needed to keep Saxon invaders at bay and hints at the terror those invaders inspired.

Clash of arms might seem distant today when gazing across Portchester harbour at the myriad of yachts, but not when walking on Hadrian's Wall on a dark winter's day. The Wall, striding on the crest of the Whin Sill, was built by a determined band of men working to precise orders, many perhaps wishing to be elsewhere. Were Roman soldiers susceptible to the common cold? Is this why soldiers imported wine mixed with horehound, a noted cough cure? This detail of life on the cold northern frontier is revealed by a Greek inscription on an amphora fragment found at the fort of Carpow.

Sterile remains on sites or areas covered with modern buildings are given imaginative treatment by reconstructions. Alan Sorrell's drawings of the Bath temple complex show one man's vision, Peter Connolly's interpretations of the military reveal another; both give life to artefacts exhibited in museums. On their own, museum exhibits may make little impression; imaginative arranging creates reality: pottery containing food, a clay pot on a gridiron with a few sticks under it showing a method of cooking. This might be supplemented by evidence from elsewhere in the empire, perhaps by a photograph of the stove in the house of the Vettii in Pompeii, where pans on tripods were left when the inhabitants ran away as the ash of Vesuvius rained down. Analysis of the contents showed that fish stew had been on the luncheon menu in August AD 79.

The Museum of Antiquities, Newcastle upon Tyne, presents reconstructions of armour as worn by legionaries and auxiliaries; close by are the original remains. The reconstructed armour proved that the bands of metal could move easily causing no problem to soldiers performing tasks such as those portrayed on Trajan's Column.

Visits to museums show the wealth of material available and also the wealth of Roman Britain in a monetary sense – a hoard of jewellery from Snettisham, another of silver from Water Newton, the Mildenhall silver tableware and hoards of coins, many once buried for safety in an insecure world. Individual coins can date a site. Coins disseminate news and are used as propaganda by emperors. Claudius celebrated his conquest of Britain by issuing coins bearing the legend *De Britann(is)*. Sometimes coins are expressive of pious hope: *Concordia Militum* (Goodwill among the soldiers) may not indicate the exact truth.

Many exhibits in museums came to light by chance finds, some by treasure hunting. Others, the result of painstaking excavation, reveal their original setting. Reconstructed wallplaster from Verulamium (St Albans) suggests the colouring and patterning required by householders. Excavations at Fishbourne, West Sussex, indicate how a garden was planted, while the mosaics suggest the artistic taste of owners of the property. They also reveal a method of construction, for when a new mosaic was required, a second one was laid on top of the first. The mosaicist may have left his trademark in the form of a bird on one mosaic. If we want to visualize the appearance of the man we might visit the mock-up of the workshop constructed in the Corinium Museum, Cirencester, or have had the good fortune to have watched the competent methods of modern Italian craftspeople.

Re-creation of the past entails careful observation of the objects, allied to modern reconstructions or parallel modern occupations. On a recent visit to Pakistan the author watched a man, squatting on the ground, pounding grain in a huge mortar and rubbing fleshy fruit in what appeared to be a bowl similar to a mortarium. The scene seemed not unlike one which might have been seen in Roman Britain.

Epigraphy provides further details. A moment in time is fixed when inscriptions record the fact that the Wroxeter forum in Shropshire was built during the reign of the Emperor Hadrian or that the first Verulamium forum was the result of an order from Agricola. Tombstones provide human details of the anguish of the final parting: at Carvoran on Hadrian's Wall, Aurelius Marcus mourned his 'very pure wife who lived 33 years without blemish', while the domestic tragedy of a tribune at the Birdoswald fort is recorded by the loss of his son aged one year and five days. Great ages on tombstones may rouse suspicion. Did Julia Secundina, the wife of Julius Valens, a veteran of the Second Augustan Legion, who died at Caerleon (Gwent), really know that her husband was aged 100 and did her son know that she was 75?

Inscriptions and graffiti are found on other media – tiles, glass, amphorae. Details can be terse but revealing. Curse tablets at Bath express the frustration of those who have had things stolen from them, wooden writing tablets provide evidence of economic transactions; advertising methods appear on clay stamps.

All this can be supplemented by literature, historical commentaries, biographies, panegyrics, poetry and letters. Some need interpretation. Caesar's account of his expeditions in the first century BC must be viewed as part of an attempt to impress his critics and supporters in Rome; Dio Cassius (died *c.* AD 235) and Tacitus re-create scenes they never saw and the latter is intent on criticizing the decadence he feels afflicts the empire. Strabo's selective geographical account of the first centuries BC and AD, a fragment of what once existed, is invaluable in creating a framework into which can be placed social, economic and political matters.

Some history, such as the Claudian invasion, is well documented, as are events like the Boudiccan rebellion, which can be supplemented by archaeology. There is, however, a danger that such periods, by the abundance of the evidence, will have too much emphasis. If Tacitus had not written a biography of his father-in-law, would Agricola's governorship have been given much prominence? Other eras tantalize by their lack of literary evidence. Libanius, a fourth-century writer, records that in AD 343 the Emperor Constans crossed to Britain in mid-winter, 'with everything, clouds, cold and swell, roused to total fury by the weather'. One can only speculate why the emperor did this.

This book attempts to give a general picture of the civilian social life which would be found in Roman Britain, by considering the archaeological evidence and interpreting it against the historical and social background. Comparative material from other parts of the empire, together with literary evidence, can supplement this. The Romans purported to govern their empire as a total whole with a single administration and law code. Yet within that empire were diversities of people, systems and products, which allowed differing patterns of behaviour.

In Britain there was a gradual change from tribal societies dominated by a native warrior aristocracy to divisions indicated more by social differentiation based on wealth and culture. Some people accepted Roman ways, others ignored or had little knowledge of them. Indigenous people mingled with those who came to Britain for a variety of reasons, bringing with them different ideas and customs. Consideration of life-styles is therefore the theme of this book rather than one Romano-British life-style.

1

Administration and society

Introduction

In two consecutive years, 55 and 54 BC, Julius Caesar invaded Britain, attempting to conquer a land situated so tantalizingly on the edge of the known Roman world. His arrival brought him into contact with the tribes of the Trinovantes, who inhabited Essex, and the Catuvellauni in Hertfordshire. The former tried to draw Caesar on to their side and his intervention certainly led to the temporary subjection of their enemies.

Caesar withdrew, basking in the glory of being the first Roman to cross Oceanus and return. He may have believed that the campaign in Britain was complete and that as promises of tribute had been given others could exploit his contacts. But civil strife in Rome and other matters consequent upon the foundation of the empire delayed the formal creation of a province.

Britain was an island of tribes (**1**). For centuries a trickle of people and full-scale movements had crossed the Channel, the latest being that of the Celtic Iron Age groups. While their way of life had impressed itself upon a more indigenous Bronze Age stock in the south, in the north a much older culture remained dominant. Roman administration was to make use of tribal groupings, all of whom had to come to terms with Rome.

For a hundred years conflict was to be postponed, but trouble flared after AD 40 when Cunobelin, King of the Catuvellauni, died, and his two sons, Togodumnus and Caratacus, decided to expand their father's domain. The

1 *Map of Britain showing the main tribal areas at the time of the Roman invasion.*

Emperor Gaius (Caligula), having toyed briefly with a plan of invasion, instead awarded himself a monument to a non-existent visit. Attacks on the Dobunni and the Atrebates upset the tribal balance and when their king, the pro-Roman Verica, fled to Claudius seeking help he found a willing listener.

Claudius, regarded by his mother as a fool and 'a man, whom Mother Nature had begun to work upon and then flung aside', had become emperor in AD 41 by chance survival and the acclamation of the Praetorian Guard (2). Physically imperfect, mentally active, he needed some military exploit to establish himself. Thoughtfully scanning a map of the empire and reviewing his resources, his eye may have alighted on Britain. Conquest beyond Oceanus would give the opportunity to complete the work of Julius Caesar and ally himself with a supreme military commander.

Troops were available with Augustus' reorganization of the army, and invading Britain might direct their abundant energy towards consolidating the empire rather than menacing their emperor. The staff work had been done by Gaius and presumably a plan of campaign was available. Invasion might also curb the power of the Druids, whose existence had been banned in Gaul by both Tiberius and Claudius because of their addiction to human sacrifice and their control of the young aristocratic class.

But no excuse was needed. The history of Rome is that of an expanding empire, and Britain, visible from the coast of Gaul, would seem its natural extension. Roman writers indicate that Rome's destiny was to be ruler of the world. Virgil (died 19 BC) made Jupiter declare, 'I set upon the Romans neither bounds of space nor of time.' Rome should rule all peoples, impose the ways of peace, spare the defeated but crush proud men who would not submit. Livy (died AD 17) stated bluntly: 'The city of Rome shall be the capital of all the world. . . . no men nor power shall be able to resist the military might of Rome.' The conquest of Britain was inevitable in the progress of Roman history.

The invasion took place under the command of Aulus Plautius, a former governor of Pannonia, who brought with him four legions and supporting auxiliary, numbering about 40,000. The Britons were no match for hardened battle-trained troops. Plautius, as no doubt he had been instructed, ensured that Claudius came to Britain to receive in person the Britons' surrender. Claudius exploited his conquest by taking the title 'Britannicus' and struck commemorative coins. He ignored Caesar's work, for a triumphal arch erected in Rome proclaimed that Claudius had accepted the surrender of eleven British kings and 'was the first to bring the barbarian peoples across the ocean under the power of the Roman state' (3). Two of the kings might have been Prasutagus of the Iceni and Cogidubnus of the Atrebates. Claudius' triumph was all he could have wished. Witnessed by 'several exiles', presumably from Britain, he rode in a decorated chariot, followed by his wife, Messalina, and the generals whose hard fighting had made this glorious day possible.

2 *Bronze head of Claudius, possibly part of a statue erected at Colchester, Essex. The head had been hacked off and may have been carted off as loot during the Boudiccan rebellion.*

3 *The remaining part of an inscription found in Rome, and now in the courtyard of the Palazzo dei Conservatori, which was once part of the triumphal arch erected by Claudius commemorating his conquest of Britain.*

Britain's value to Rome

The Romans incorporated Britain as a province, but fierce resistance by the northern tribes meant that any intention by the Romans of conquering the whole island had to be abandoned. The building of Hadrian's Wall (**colour plate 1**) and for a short time the occupation of the Antonine Wall meant that a boundary had been placed on the northern frontiers of the empire.

In spite of vicious rebellions, such as that led by Boudicca in AD 60–1, and attempts by usurpers to seize power, Britain remained an integral part of the empire. The island was useful as a repository for troops who could be kept occupied on a frontier region. Tacitus claims that the Britons readily submitted to recruitment in the army and other obligations 'imposed by the government so long as there are no abuses'; these men could be used to man the frontiers elsewhere.

The number of the army has been estimated at about 55,000 at its greatest extent, dropping later to about 20,000 out of a total population in Britain of over three million. Its impact was mainly felt in the frontier regions and at places where its spending power helped the local economy. Dependants of liaisons and (after Septimius Severus' reforms of AD 197) legalized marriages, civilians living near or having contact with the forts, and veterans, who retired in the province, acted as instruments of Romanization. By the end of the period, however, it is probable that the reverse was happening and that the army was becoming increasingly Celticized.

Britain was exploited for gold, silver and other metals, 'the price of victory' according to Tacitus. Later she provided huge quantities of grain, especially in the fourth century for the Emperor Julian's Rhineland campaign. Overall, however, Rome probably did not gain from Britain as much as she expected, although Britain benefited from trading experience, which brought in new products and commercial expertise.

Law and administration systems bound Britain to Rome and extended the career pattern of men aspiring to civil and military office. These gained valuable experience and contributed to imposing an organized form of government in the island. In religion, apart from their dislike of the Druids, Roman tolerance allowed pagan, Oriental and Classical worship and belief to exist and, it might be argued, provided a more humane belief in the form of Christianity.

For 400 years, Britain was part of an empire, which integrated its life-style with that already present in Britain among the Celtic tribes. While some parts were hardly touched by Roman influence, elsewhere the promotion of urban centres provided sound local government, amenities which Rome considered to be the basis of a civilized life, and living standards akin to those expected by a citizen of a great empire. These standards extended to villa owners many of whom, by the fourth century, occupied luxurious houses supported by the wealth of their carefully managed estates.

How far Britain followed a Romanized way of life is debatable. In the early years of the twentieth century historical consideration was undoubtedly influenced by a view of an imperial past. Francis Haverfield in 1906, for example, considered Rome brought civilizing ways to Britain. Reconsideration has meant that in the 1990s emphasis focuses on the tenacious survival of native customs and the ability of the Celtic elite to make terms with Rome, themes perhaps influenced by modern reaction to western imperialism and consideration given to the importance of native populations. The fusion of two societies is a complex social process with interaction occurring at different levels and in response to differing human needs. Out of this interaction emerged a society perhaps better described more as Romano-Celtic than as Romano-British.

Pre-Roman society

Any society is composed of a variety of social groupings, which remain static until change results from emerging ideas or, more abruptly, because a different societal structure imposes itself bringing new rules and cultural patterns. But unless there is a rigid totalitarian regime, the societal pattern gradually alters as people adapt themselves to the new order while retaining many of their former characteristics. This reflects the situation in Britain after AD 43, especially in the first two centuries, when absorption into the Roman empire created tensions as Celtic tribal society, especially the aristocratic elite, came to terms with a Roman hierarchical structure.

In Pre-Roman Britain, Celtic tribal society was dominated by chieftains who acted as political leaders, although the career of the Icenian queen, Boudicca, indicates that a woman could lead her followers into battle, while Cartumandua's rule was sufficiently important for the Romans to keep her on the Brigantian throne for a generation after the conquest. After AD 43 many chieftains became dependable client rulers. Cogidubnus, King of the Atrebates, ensured his tribe's loyalty to Rome and provided a base from which the southern coast could be overrun.

Caesar's description of society in Gaul may indicate the situation in Britain. He states that below the chiefs or kings were the Druids with religious and judicial functions, and the knights, whose position and power depended on the number of retainers who served them. Then came the common people, who were neither consulted nor acted on their own initiative. Tribal rivalry and the quarrels of the nobles led to political instability, a situation which replicated itself in Britain allowing the Romans to ensure the loyalty of one tribe while subduing another.

Caesar also mentions a group which may have owed services to a lord who acted as protector and patron. This service was mainly agricultural, but held in great respect were craftsmen, especially metalworkers, whose intricate work was essential to a warrior society. Graves discovered in the Yorkshire Wolds reveal a wealthy military society buried with their weapons and chariots. Celtic Ireland had a similar society where poets extolled the close bonds existing between chieftains and their charioteers. Caesar had noted the tactics of chariot warfare but, by the time of the Claudian invasion, this method of fighting had become obsolete.

Evidence from sites such as Little Woodbury in Wiltshire suggests that farming families gathered behind defended enclosures, raising crops, breeding cattle and storing grain in pits during the winter months. This reflects Caesar's description of the Celts fortifying large circular enclosures with felled trees to make huts and cattle pens. Larger enclosures like Danebury in Hampshire provided permanently defended community settlements while others, especially in the northern areas, would relate to a more nomadic society, moving cattle from lowland winter grazing areas to summer hill pasturage.

Large hill-forts, especially in southern Britain, suggest a society under the control of local aristocracy as equally restless and riven by powerful factions as in Gaul, with the hill-forts forming centres for tribal allegiance, a rallying place in time of war, a meeting-place in time of peace. This aristocracy was already taking advantage of a more ostentatious Roman civilization. Tombs at Lexden, Essex, and Welwyn, Hertfordshire, contained Roman pottery and silverware; a settlement at Hengistbury Head in Dorset was trading in Roman wine, glass, pottery and using Gallic coins as a medium of exchange. Profits from trade would be a dominant factor in securing compliance from merchants, while it was from the ranks of the aristocracy, emulating Roman life-styles, that Rome would draw its local administration, relying on its experience in ruling tribal groupings to encourage obedience to the new regime.

A multi-cultural society

After the conquest local administration was based on towns, small by modern standards, their populations ranging from 2000 to 15,000. Sometimes, as in the case of Maiden Castle, Dorset, the inhabitants were moved from a hillfort (**colour plate 2**) into a new town to ensure that they were kept under observation and to initiate them into a Romanized way of life.

But the majority of the population probably continued to follow rural pursuits. Many places, especially in Wales, the Cornish peninsula and the northern areas, would be comparatively untouched by Roman rule. In Northumberland excavation has shown that generation after generation were rebuilding houses surrounded by stone walls, raising livestock and keeping out of the way of the authorities. Only in the third century AD did something akin to civic feeling emerge. An inscription refers to the *civitas* of the Carvetii centred in the Eden valley in Cumbria and probably having a link with Carlisle.

Some people gained sufficient wealth to build accommodation emulating Classical architectural forms, leading to the development of the villa with enhanced comfort conditions. They might copy the habits of neighbours, possibly official administrators or newly retired veterans. But transference of ideas is a subtle process. One generation may refuse to accept what it considers to be aspects of an alien culture; the next adapts more easily to a more modern attitude. More comfortable advantages of villa life and amenities of urbanization were adopted, not necessarily to indicate Romanized habits but because they brought a higher standard of living.

Other factors affected the development of society. In the first century Roman law distinguished between *peregrini* and Roman citizens, but citizenship was gradually given to individuals and communities, so that towns with the title of *municipium* could be granted citizenship *en masse*, as perhaps happened at Verulamium. After Caracalla's decree of AD 212 all were citizens of one empire.

The huge military presence included not only men from Italy and the more Romanized provinces of the empire but also auxiliaries from Gaul, Spain, Batavia, Thrace, the German frontier regions, North Africa and the Near East. Intermarriage was common throughout society. The merchant Barates from Palmyra, a dealer in military flags or ensigns, married his former slave-girl, Regina, from the Celtic Catuvellaunian tribe (**4**). Julia Fortunata was a loyal wife to the *Sevir Augustalis*, Marcus Verecundius Diogenes. She came from Sardinia, he from Bituriges Cubi (Bourges) in Aquitania; both died at York (**5**).

Social mobility meant that Italian administrators, Greek teachers and doctors, Gallic sculptors and Near Eastern merchants, visited and settled in Britain. By the end of the fourth century German mercenaries, brought by Theodosius to stiffen the coastal defences, were residing in the Nene valley around Peterborough, or were being buried at Dorchester-on-Thames. Saxons were soon to join them. The appearance of these groups added yet another strand woven into the

4 *The tombstone of Regina, who died at South Shields aged only thirty, is representative of the intermarriage which could take place in Britain. The merchant Barates, from Palmyra, married his former slave-girl, Regina, from the Celtic Catuvellaunian tribe. Under the Latin inscription are words in Palmyrene which restrainedly express his grief: 'Regina, the freedwoman of Barates, alas.'*

social structure of Romano-British society, to which the term 'multi-cultural' may be appropriately applied.

The governor

Britain was administered by a legate with military authority designated to him by the emperor. Such a man was a senator, having property of over one million sesterces, who had served as one of the two consuls in Rome and was thus confident of his own authority to rule. Posted to Britain, which had a reputation of being a difficult province with its northern tribes still unsubdued, he would also have had experience of administration in other provinces.

Tacitus' biography of his father-in-law, Agricola, indicates that the governor's duties extended beyond those of a military nature. Before he came to Britain Agricola had been governor of Aquitania, a peaceful province giving him experience in civil administration. In Britain his duties included administering justice, seeking out wrongdoers, curtailing the over-zealous attitude of some of his subordinate officials and, most importantly, showing the visible presence of the authority of Rome. Tacitus comments that in his first year of office (in AD 77–8) Agricola stopped certain corrupt practices and both privately and with official assistance encouraged the building of temples, public squares and private houses.

5 *Another example of a marriage of people from different parts of the empire. The coffin of Julia Fortunata, born in Sardinia, wife to the* Sevir Augustalis, *Marcus Verecundius Diogenes.*

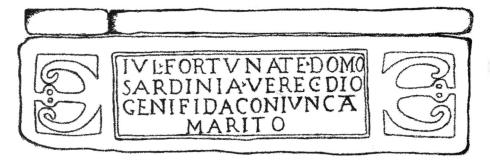

Some of his staff were permanent: clerks, secretaries and other bureaucratic staff processed the vast amount of information which entered and left their offices. *Beneficarii*, seconded from military units, organized supplies and maintained roads and as a group might form a guild for companionship; an inscription mentioning the restoration of their clubhouse has been found at York. *Speculatores* acted as guards to prisoners, gave information on suspected criminals, made arrests and saw that sentences given by magistrates were carried out. Their zeal was ensured by the fact that they could claim a criminal's goods after his execution.

In addition, the governor brought his own friends and staff with him. Tacitus is careful to tell us that Agricola was influenced neither by personal feelings nor recommendations, with the underlying implication that many others were. Nor did Agricola employ freedmen or slaves whose loyalty might lie elsewhere. Even so, his information system functioned most efficiently; he 'knew everything, though he did not act as if he did know'.

The procurator

Such a man, however, backed by almost absolute authority and a superb fighting machine, might become dangerous, so the emperor delegated authority to other officials on a system of divide and rule. A procurator was appointed from the *equites*, an independent agent, who, reporting directly to the emperor, was responsible for administering finance, collecting taxes and levying grain to feed the army. He might be a freedman or a retired centurion, who had saved enough money to gain admittance to the class of the *equites* by buying property above 400,000 sesterces. Probably the most famous procurator in history is Pontius Pilate, who, for an ill-starred moment, was Procurator of Judea.

One of the most humane procurators in Britain was Julius Classicianus, a provincial of Celtic descent, whose previous service commanding a cavalry regiment in Britain and his marriage to Julia Pacata, the daughter of a Celtic noble in the Trier region, ensured that he mitigated the harsh treatment being put on the battle-scarred province after the Boudiccan rebellion, by the governor, Suetonius Paulinus (**6**). Other officials with the title of procurator administered imperial estates, mines and weaving factories.

Subordinate officers under the control of the procurator were the censors, who kept the taxation records up to date. Only two have their names recorded in Britain, one dealing with the inhabitants of Colchester, the other with those of Annandale in south-west Scotland.

The law officer (*legatus iuridicus*)

The governor administered civil and criminal law throughout the province in all cases concerning Roman citizens, but he did not administer native law, although he could hear appeals from decisions made under that system. A Roman citizen could appeal to Rome, as did Paul of Tarsus, in which case he would have to go there in order to put his case before the emperor. To assist the governor a law officer was appointed, who would be particularly useful when the governor was away on campaigns. One such was Marcus Vettius Valens, who later became a patron of Britain, a post to which he was elected as a man with sufficient influence in Rome to promote the interests of the province.

The provincial council

Each province had a provincial council composed of delegates from the tribal areas, whose main duty was to swear allegiance to the emperor on behalf of their people. If the British council was similar to that established in Gaul, its act of loyalty was accompanied by a festival. It exerted moral pressure on the governor and the law officer since commendations and criticisms were sent to Rome when their respective terms of office ended. By the end of the second century the council seems to have ensured that law codes were enforced and, rather surprisingly, checked the number of teachers and doctors who were working in the province.

19

6 *Tombstone of Gaius Julius Alpinus Classicianus, who was sent as procurator to Britain in AD 61, erected by his wife, Julia Pacata, daughter of Julius Indus, a Celtic noble in the Trier region.*

Town government

Each town was administered by an *ordo*, elected from male, wealthy property owners. That in the *coloniae*, established for retired veterans, was expected to provide a role-model, but, though

Tacitus stated that Colchester (Essex) was founded to acquaint the natives with law-abiding government, he had to admit that the aggressive behaviour of the colonists was one of the reasons why the Trinovantes rose in revolt.

Slightly lower in status were *municipia*, which had a charter giving Latin civic rights and also incorporating native law. Citizenship could be granted to those who were willing to become members of the town council, taking on the trappings of office and paying for the provision of amenities from their own pocket. If they could not afford to do so there were always Romans such as Seneca ready to lend money.

Within the council two senior officials tried petty crimes and civil cases and supervised public ceremonies. Every fourth year they ensured vacancies in the council were filled. An unpopular duty was to reassess public taxation and they also negotiated contracts for public buildings. Two junior officials were responsible for the upkeep of those public buildings and amenities in the town, paying for them out of their own pocket.

A third group of towns, the *civitas*-capitals, was established as administrative centres for tribal groups. A deliberate policy, which had been successful in Gaul, brought the Durotriges from the hill-fort of Maiden Castle to Dorchester and promoted the native settlement of the Cantiaci at Canterbury. There was yet a fourth group, known as *vici*, which developed piecemeal for a variety of reasons. Some, like Godmanchester, might be service stations along a main road; others grew under the protection of a fort, as did Housesteads on Hadrian's Wall.

Changes in central administration

The system of central administration lasted throughout the first two centuries, but sometime after AD 197 the province was divided, possibly by the Emperor Caracalla. Most of lowland Britain became *Britannia Superior*, with a governor of consular rank because it had two legions, the Twentieth at Chester and the Second Augusta at Caerleon. His headquarters were probably at London. A governor of lesser rank was in charge

of the rest of Britain, including the garrisons on Hadrian's Wall, at Lincoln and at York, where he most likely made his headquarters. A more drastic change, which was part of the almost total reorganization of the empire after it had been a battleground for usurpers and pretenders, came at the end of the third century. Britain had broken away from the empire for some of the time and so had to be more carefully controlled.

The empire was now ruled by two emperors, Diocletian and Maximian. Maximian and his deputy, Constantius, ruled the western part of the empire and created Britain as a diocese within the Praetorian Prefecture of Gaul. The governor of Britain, given the title *vicarius*, was responsible to that prefect, and to ensure tighter control Britain was divided into four provinces. *Britannia Prima* in the south-west seems to have had its capital at Cirencester (Glos.), where a fourth-century inscription on the base of a giant column mentions its erection by L. Septimius, who describes himself as *praeses* of *Britannia Prima* and combined the duties of legate and procurator.

Maxima Caesariensis covered the south-east with its capital in London; the area of *Britannia Secunda* included the Wall garrison with its headquarters at York. The fourth province, *Flavia Caesariensia*, was centred on Lincoln. Later the name *Valencia* appears, which may have been an alternative name for one of the provinces, or was perhaps a fifth province, variously placed in Wales, the Scottish Lowlands and the north-west.

This reorganization also included the division of the civil and military authorities. The governor now dealt entirely with civilian functions, while new military commanders, with titles of *dux* and *comes*, commanded sections of the army and, in particular, fought the barbarians who were attacking the province. The Counts of the Saxon Shore had a hard task and in AD 367 barbarian raiders killed one of them, Nectaridus, while at the same time Fullofaudes, *Dux Britanniarum*, had to fight desperately when he was ambushed somewhere in the west.

The inhabitants of Britain were uneasily aware that the empire was beginning to fail them. It was barbarians with Roman names, now vested with authority, who controlled frontier regions with the approval of the central authority. Little support came from the official garrisons, which had gradually been depleted. After AD 401 the Sixth and the Second Augustan Legions were withdrawn from what was becoming an increasingly apprehensive Britain.

The end of Roman administration

On the last day of December AD 406, in a bitterly cold winter, the Rhine froze over. Across it poured the Vandals, Alans and Suebi to spread over Gaul. Britain was experiencing problems with usurpers and during the resulting chaos the Saxons, according to the Byzantine historian Zosimos, 'overran everything at will reducing the inhabitants of Britain to the necessity of rebelling from the Roman empire and living by themselves no longer obeying Roman laws'. This may be interpreted either as a revolt against what remained of the administration or as an attempt at order by civilians trying desperately to fend for themselves. Three years later the cities of Britain appealed to the emperor, but to no avail. Honorius could only tell them they must defend themselves. From that moment official administration by Rome ceased.

Unofficial leaders made their appearance from time to time. When Germanus, Bishop of Auxerre, came to Verulamium in 429, local administration had not broken down for he was received by leading citizens, 'distinguished by their riches, resplendent in their attire and surrounded by the adulation of the multitude'. If the stout walls of Verulamium protected a competent administration there was chaos elsewhere. Germanus, an ex-army officer, was persuaded to fight off a raiding party of Picts and Saxons, who fled on hearing the battlecry, 'Alleluia'.

Already Saxons were settling in Kent and East Anglia resisting all attempts to expel them. They shattered the fragile economy, wreaking such disaster that in AD 446 a despairing letter was sent to Aetius, military commander of the emperor, Valentinian III: 'To Aetius, thrice consul, the barbarians drive us to the sea, the sea to the barbarians. Between these two modes of death we are killed or drowned.' And to be killed or drowned was their fate for, so far as we know, their anguished cry went unanswered. The great empire, which had once been Rome, had her own problems and was content for the provinces to seek their own destiny.

Slavery

Slavery was accepted as a natural part of society in the Celtic and Classical worlds. Persons captured in battle or condemned for a criminal offence lost their freedom and became a trading commodity. Strabo classified them casually as one of the goods exported from pre-Roman Britain to Gaul. After the conquest there must have been huge numbers enslaved in Britain and this would continue after rebellions in the first century. Caesar also noted that because of heavy taxes some people deliberately made themselves slaves of the nobility.

In the ancient world it was accepted that all freeborn men and women were a distinct category from slaves, who might have little or no personality and were regarded as property to be bought and sold at will. Aristotle refers to a slave, in a chilling phrase, as a 'vocal tool'. In the republic slaves had been subject to humiliating punishments and were at the receiving end of a great deal of cruelty. During the empire conditions improved; by the second century AD masters were forbidden to sell slaves to be torn by the beasts in the amphitheatre and any master who slew a slave might be accused of homicide.

A slave society is a form of conspicuous consumption where labour is wasted on menial tasks; slaves might act as lantern bearers, scavengers and even as clocks to call the hours. Lucian, writing in the mid-second century, remarks that slaves walked before fashionable Romans in the street to point out obstacles; others used a slave to greet their friends for them. Slaves carrying out these pointless tasks were better off than those who were condemned to the quarries and the mines. Despite the emergence of Christian radical

thinking which stressed the brotherhood of man and the equality of slave and master, early bishoprics and monastic houses kept slaves.

Slaves were fortunate if they lived in a household or an establishment which treated them according to the law. Sometimes, if offered their freedom, they might prefer to remain with the family which gave them food and shelter. Well-educated slaves, especially Greeks, became tutors, bookkeepers or estate managers. Pliny the Younger treated the better educated of his slaves as equals, encouraging them to discuss intellectual matters.

Attachment between master and slaves
Sincere attachment between master and slave might continue after a slave had been manumitted and become the equal of any free citizen. Numerianus, a trooper of the first cavalry of Asturians, so appreciated his freedman, Victor, who died aged twenty at South Shields (Tyne and Wear), that he erected a magnificent tombstone to him. Tombstones mentioning *alumni* or foster children may be indicative of slave children. Some had been foundlings; others, adopted into households, acted as companions to young children. Slaves could marry freeborn citizens although the married partner might then take slave status, as possibly did Claudia Martina, who married Anencletus, a slave of the provincial council; this 'devoted wife' died aged only nineteen. Some slaves were encouraged by their masters to become specialists in a trade; one, trained as a goldsmith, dedicated an altar at Norton near Malton (N. Yorks.).

Unpleasant work
Slaves would be responsible for some of the most unpleasant jobs in Britain – working in the

7 A slave gang-chain from Llyn Cerrig Bach, Anglesey.

mines, the docks and on the imperial estates. For some life would be brutish and short, indeed very short, if the large number of infant burials at the Hambleden villa represents the offspring of slaves. The owners might be expected to rear such children to sell them for profit, but this meant bearing the expense until they were of marketable age. Lack of good hygiene could also contribute to these premature deaths.

Ill-treatment included being put in chains, as had been done in the pre-Roman Iron Age (7). Large neck rings interlocked into rings looped one over the other prevented slaves from running away as they trudged to and from the fields to work. Thick ropes were also used for restraint. Two small bronze figurines, one from Brough (Cumbria) and the other from London, depict seated slaves with ropes tied round their necks, dropping to go round their hands and thence to the feet (8). The poignant condition of all slaves is personified by the figure of the weary and pathetic slave sitting waiting for his master, designed as a *balsamarium* and found at Aldborough (9). Slaves joined a guild since membership provided some form of social life and mutual assistance. By law a master had to bury his slaves but if he evaded this the guild ensured that this was done and that the correct rites were performed at the burial and on the anniversary of death.

Women slaves
Women, especially, had a hard life. They might be sold to produce children, who became the property of the master. He could sleep with her at will and sue any other man who did this as violator of his personal property. She married only

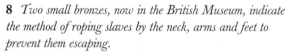

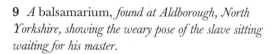

8 *Two small bronzes, now in the British Museum, indicate the method of roping slaves by the neck, arms and feet to prevent them escaping.*

9 *A* balsamarium, *found at Aldborough, North Yorkshire, showing the weary pose of the slave sitting waiting for his master.*

with his permission; Martial (died *c.* AD 104) satirizes the master who sells his slave mistress and then buys her back because he cannot bear to be without her. Many female slaves worked in brothels or in the mines. A household slave, at the whim of her mistress, could spend hours intricately curling, or plaiting the hair. A relief from Neumagen, Germany, shows one maid doing this, while another resignedly holds the mirror and two wait to offer required perfumes (**10**).

It was not unusual for people to be sold as slaves. Regina, the freedwoman who married Barates, seems to have suffered the fate of many children. In the late second century there seems to have been no particular reason why members of the Catuvellaunian tribe should have been enslaved, so she may have been sold by her parents into slavery. Pirate raids must have been dreaded; one of their victims in the fourth century was the future St Patrick. Another victim was

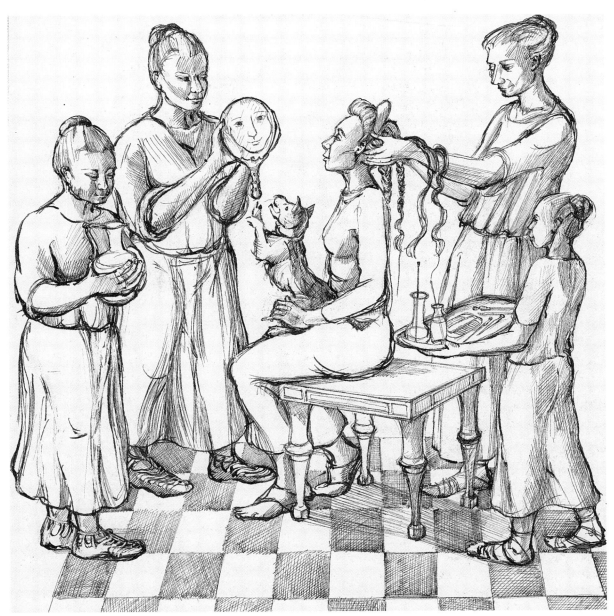

10 *Women household slaves attending to their mistress's toilet.*

recorded in a law case. Pirates captured a woman working in the salt-mines, somewhere in Britain, and sold her to Marcus Cocceius Firmus, whose centurional service in the Second Augustan Legion is recorded on inscriptions at Auchendavy (Strathclyde). When the authorities found out, she was returned to the mines leaving the centurion to sue the imperial treasury for refund of her purchase price. She might have preferred the colder air of the Antonine Wall region to the toil of the mines, but neither her wishes, nor those of her new master, were of any importance.

Freedmen

Freedmen had another status and could rise to high rank in civilian posts. From Phrygia in Tricomia, an inscription to M. Aurelius Marcio

25

records a varied career as successively manager of slate marble quarries, procurator of the province of Britain and manager of the scenery and stage props for theatres of the capital, a juxta-position of posts obviously requiring organization skills. Other men served the military; Verecundus and Novicius erected a tombstone to the centu-rion Marcus Favonius Facilis at Colchester. Some went into trade, others into industry. Anthony Birley suggests that five potters at the same work-shop of Colchester, all named Sextus Valerius but with different cognomina, set up in business after manumission. If so, their excellent business for nearly thirty years supplied products to the southern and eastern coasts of Britain.

Education: Celtic oral tradition

When the Romans arrived in Britain they were meeting a civilization which encouraged learning and believed in the transmission of understand-ing between master and pupil by oral means. Caesar remarked that students of Druidism spent up to twenty years on their studies and that, though the Druids used the Greek alphabet, oral learning enabled them to prevent their doctrines from becoming public property as well as training the memory, 'for when people have the help of texts, they are less diligent in learning by heart and let their memories rust'.

People who rely on oral tradition develop an ability to retain knowledge, which is passed on in methodical and repetitive form. Poetry, especially epic verse, is an easy method of committing material to memory by the chanting of rhymed couplets. There is a natural repetition and logical-ity which is easy for a speaker to declaim and a listener to remember. The imagination is keener because it is allowed to develop unchecked and some sort of mental shorthand results where lis-teners, knowing what is to come, fill out knowledge for themselves. Throughout Celtic Europe there was evidence for a flourishing oral prose and poetic tradition, which was conveyed in vivid imagery and language.

Yet the evidence for some form of written tra-dition is there, judging by Caesar's remarks about the Greek language. There is also Strabo's comment that 'if won over by persuasion the Gauls devoted their energies to gentle pursuits and even take to a literary education'. The evi-dence for this is somewhat limited but Celtic coins had names on them and pieces of pottery are marked with graffiti. If a people have no use for written texts they do not create or use them. It was when the Celts came into contact with the Roman world that they found themselves at a disadvantage with a civilization which had devel-oped an enormous literary heritage and, most importantly, the means by which written commu-nication was both easy and cheap.

Formal learning

This disadvantage could be overcome. The Celts were quick learners and the upper classes valued new methods which aided them in communicat-ing ideas and boosting their wealth through trade. Tacitus' remark that Agricola trained the sons of chieftains with a liberal education is a reminder of a two-way process. If the Celts saw the benefit of formal learning, the Romans also perceived an advantage in training future leaders. The Boudiccan rebellion probably convinced the government that they had neglected this aspect of Romanization. The sons may also have been made hostage for the good faith of their fathers, a practice familiar to both Celts and Romans. But Agricola was appreciative of what Tacitus referred to as a British natural ability. Possibly a supply of trained teachers came from Rome, skilled in communicating ideas, so that soon 'a dislike of the Latin language was replaced by a passion to speak it' (11).

Writing tablets

Literary texts were studied from a papyrus roll but as this was many feet in length it was awk-ward to use and easily damaged, especially if reference was made back and forth along the text. For this reason the master read aloud pas-sages adding his own comments and encouraging learning by heart, a method which held no ter-rors for pupils brought up in an oral tradition.

11 *A Romano-British schoolroom. One boy reads from a scroll, another works at his desk using a stylus on a wax tablet.*

One fragment of papyrus was found at Verulamium, but there is evidence for the other method of documentation, the writing tablet. This was a wooden flat surface with a raised edge placed round it to contain wax poured into the shallow box. The tablet was folded, wax side to wax side, to form a book. A cord, wrapped round it, was sealed to ensure privacy. Wax was then poured into a metal box with loops at the side and corners through which the ends of the cords could pass. The wax was stamped with a seal and the box was closed. A lozenge-shaped box was found at Nettleton but round or square-shaped ones were more common.

The pointed end of a stylus scratched a message on to the wax; the flattened or rounded end smoothed out words. Several examples from London reveal the variety of decorated ends available to writers. When the stylus was pressed very hard it cut into the wood, leaving therein marks which allow the archaeologist to decipher the letters. Some of the Vindolanda tablets were written directly with ink on to thin slices of boxwood and were linked together by ties put through holes in the ends. Many refer to items of foodstuffs or to military movements, while the London examples, as might be expected, are connected with trade.

Ink, made from carbon or lampblack, was kept in a pottery or metal container. A pottery non-spill inkwell was devised so that if it tipped over an inner lip prevented spillage. Excavations in London have produced a pottery bulbous one and a pointed metal shape with a hinged lid. Pens were of reed and occasionally of metal with a thickened end to hold the ink.

Demetrius the schoolmaster

Written comments identified the contents of amphorae; at Brough-on-Noe (Derbyshire) one had contained plums (*pruna*), another at Richborough held *lympa*, a wine produced near Mount Vesuvius. These examples are from military sites but graffiti provides evidence of some education in Britain for there is little evidence of teaching. Plutarch remarks that, when he was at the Pythian festival (AD 84–5) at Delphi in Greece, he held a conversation with a schoolmaster, Demetrius of Tarsus, who dedicated a bronze plaque to the deities of the governor's headquarters in York. The governor had made the schoolmaster accompany a voyage along the western coast of Scotland and this experience probably caused him to make a dedication to Oceanus and Tethys in great thankfulness that he had survived the northern seas.

In Britain competence to read and write would enable a man to get a job as tutor in a household or to set up his private school. It might also provide him with work as a clerk in the docks of ports such as London or in a merchant's employ. In towns and villas an appreciation of higher branches of learning would exist, that is to say a familiarity with Classical texts and myths. It is perhaps significant that Celtic mythology, though portrayed in sculpture, does not appear in mosaics. Owners of villas preferred Classical stories such as Dido and Aeneas (**colour plate 3**), the myth of Orpheus or Europa and the bull.

Language

What language was spoken in Britain? Officially it was Latin but fluency in a language comes only when people unconsciously organize their thoughts in it. Latin was the normal medium of communication for administrators sent from Rome, who would also appreciate nuances of language and readings of Classical authors. Those Britons who wished to be part of the adminis-

trative structure or to have official posts probably engaged language tutors for themselves and their families.

Soldiers absorbed Latin as part of the army training; writing tablets found in London indicate that it was also the working language for trade and thus for clerks working in docks and offices. Pupils learnt Latin, probably in its purest form, as part of their education. Monumental masons and sculptors had to pick up the language very quickly, learning to carve in superb lettering, or else they would lose custom to newcomers flooding into Britain seeking work.

It is difficult to know how far Latin was the language of the people. Gildas, in the sixth century, spoke of Latin as being 'our language' (*nostra lingua*), but he was a member of an organization which used Latin as its official medium of communication, useful for its universality. Celtic names became Latinized. Tamesubugus and Cunoarda, potters in the Nene valley, Latinized their names. The latter inscribes his pottery *Cunoarda fecit vico Durobrivis* (Cunoarda made this at the settlement of Water Newton [Cambs.]). Clementinus, tilemaker at Silchester (Hants), inscribes them *fecit tubul(um) Clementinus*. These phrases might mean that manufacturers thought in Latin or that this was a convenient way of marking goods.

As Celtic communication skills lay in oral tradition, it is no surprise that people practised their writing skills in graffiti. The oft-quoted phrase from London, 'Austalis has gone off on his own every day for thirteen days' might as easily have been written by a disgruntled educated tilemaker as a Romanized Celt taking out his frustration in the new medium of writing (**12**).

In some of the wilder parts of Britain Latin could remain an alien language, with Celtic spoken in the home. In the towns a younger generation learned Latin as a matter of course, passing it on to the next generation. But the Celtic heroic tradition survived in the vernacular; Celtic mythological and heroic epics, with their constant repetition of phrase, could lose much of their attraction if told in another language.

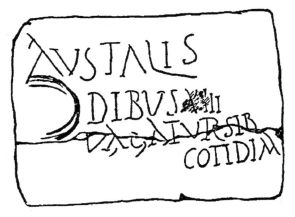

12 *Graffito found in London, 'Austalis has gone off on his own every day for thirteen days'.*

Latin might be looked upon with suspicion as a propaganda exercise. If it was not necessary to write or speak in Latin, and people could converse in a language which was second-nature, there was no need to learn Latin. The position in some areas might be the same as in Britain today where one language is spoken in school or at work, but a native language is carefully nurtured in the home. This leads to a patois developing, which might be the case in Roman Britain. In spite of Gildas's words, Britain might have had several forms of language: official Latin, Celtic dialects and a kind of hybrid-patois spoken by the majority of the population.

2

Religion, belief and death

Celtic belief

Belief and superstition are entwined in every society and Celtic acceptance of the spirit world as normal practice impressed Caesar. 'The whole Celtic race', he noted, 'is given over to religious observances', which was understandable when personal deities were identified with familiar things – stones, trees, water – and more menacing beings with unexplainable storms and floods. All stages of life needed protection, particularly at the end, when the otherworld awaited, as real as the present one. Anxiety requires religious practices for what seems unpredictable.

Celtic belief is elusive because evidence is often related secondhand through Classical or later Celtic texts. Names of deities, carved on altars and statues, reinterpret through a Classical medium and may not convey an exact meaning. Caesar said that the Gauls had images of Mercury but it is uncertain if these represented a purely Roman deity or some Celtic god with attributes similar to Mercury.

Emperor worship and the imperial cult

Roman religion, on the other hand, had evolved on political and social levels. Simple faith in the operation of divine forces was refined into a theological framework combining obedience to the State with tolerance for individual belief. This was supplemented by religions from the eastern part of the empire and eventually all beliefs were to be challenged by Christianity.

The Roman State promoted religion on a political basis by encouraging worship of the emperor and ensuring the loyalty of the army. Evidence from Dura Europos on the Euphrates indicates prescribed ceremonies connected with the birthday of a military unit and the commemoration of deities or abstract concepts such as Roma, Victoria and Disciplina. Worship was also expected from civilians. Britannia, deified as a goddess, personified the province, and townspeople were encouraged to seek the divine protection of Tyche, portrayed as a woman wearing a turreted crown. A stone statue-head found at Silchester and a relief at Lincoln indicate that at least two towns did this.

Emperor worship need not imply that emperors were worshipped in their lifetime; most were proclaimed divine after death. Suetonius reported the dying Vespasian's cynical words (died AD 79), 'Alas I am becoming a god', but Commodus (ruled 180–92) had no hesitation in identifying himself with Hercules while alive. The emperor was credited with numen, or spiritual power, and dedications to that power were made by the army and administrative officials to show their loyalty.

The imperial cult established an official centre with a massive temple at Colchester. Its dedication to the Emperor Claudius would impress on the Britons that a living god had visited them, but it so symbolized the power of Rome that it was destroyed by the Trinovantes in AD 60. Rebuilt on the same foundation, the temple dominated a large courtyard flanked by porticoed arcades. Good drainage was provided for washing away the blood of animals sacrificed at the altar placed in front of the temple steps.

Later the main centre of the cult was probably moved to London, but as an expression of loyalty to the State other cities established *Seviri Augustales,* who arranged sacrifices and festivals. No matter how stupid or evil the man, respect for his divinity as emperor ensured the continuity of respect due to the State.

The Classical pantheon

Rome had absorbed her deities from the Greek pantheon or had developed gods associated with natural phenomena or particular functions. The greatest was the triumvirate: Jupiter, Juno and Minerva. Inscriptions to Jupiter Optimus Maximus invoke the protection of both the individual and the State. Possibly a temple in each town, like those in the Verulamium forum,

13 *The forum at Verulamium. At least one temple was built in the Classical style. (Drawing by Alan Sorrell)*

contained a cult statue (**13**). An inscription reused in the building of the riverside wall at London records the restoration of a temple to him in the third century.

Certain groups required patron deities (**14**). Minerva, worshipped by warriors and craftsmen, also had healing powers, as did Apollo. Mercury (**15**) was guardian of travellers and protected merchants; Mercury and Apollo were invoked in Lincoln, seemingly by guilds, to give protection to the wards into which the city was divided. Mars, invoked by soldiers, also protected travellers. A relief at York may represent Vulcan, patron of ironworkers. Venus like Juno was

31

14 *Bronze figurines of Hercules, height 8cm (3.1in), from Cowlinge, Suffolk, and Mercury, height 16.2cm (6.4in), from Manea Fen, Lincolnshire.*

15 *A bronze figure of Mercury, height 6.1cm (2.4in), found at Richborough, Kent. Round the neck is a torc, indicating that some worshipper regarded the Roman deity as having Celtic characteristics.*

invoked by women in childbirth. The fact that so many deities had dual or even triple personalities made it easy for their functions to be understood by both Celts and Romans. The comprehensive mythology, based on aspects of life which the Celts considered vital – warfare, fertility, prosperity and the otherworld – merged with the Roman pantheon.

Celtic deities

Many Celtic deities remained local. The water nymph Coventina, who is linked to the nymphs, water goddesses, of the Roman world, presided at Carrawburgh (**16**); the deity of the River Wharfe

16 *A relief to the water goddess 'Covventina', dedicated by Titus Cosconianus, prefect of the first cohort of Batavians, found at her shrine at the fort of Carrawburgh on Hadrian's Wall. The goddess holds a water plant in her right hand and reclines on the waters flowing from the urn by her left side.*

in North Yorkshire, Verbeia, is invoked at Ilkley. Other gods covered a wider area. Warfare had been endemic to the Celts: 'The whole race', marvelled Strabo, 'is war mad.' In Brigantian territory, the warrior deities Cocidius and Belatucadrus merged in personality with Mars. Elsewhere Mars' earlier fertility aspects were invoked so that as Mars Lenus (healer) he was worshipped at Caerwent (Gwent), as Braciaca (malt or beer) in Derbyshire and as Olludius (mighty tree) at Custom Scrubs, Bisley (Glos.).

Interpretations were complex. Brigantia, tribal goddess of the Brigantes, conflated with Minerva, a warrior goddess and patron of craftsmen. She is winged on a relief at Birrens in Dumfries and Galloway, akin in symbolism to Minerva Victrix, whose official portrayal can be seen at Corbridge (Northd.). An inscription, *Dea Victoria Brigantia* at Castleford (W. Yorks.), reinforces this connection and Minerva has an association with water when she merges with the Celtic Sulis of the healing springs of Bath. Such complexities were natural to Celtic thought where the concept of shape-changing from one shadowy existence to another was accepted without question.

Celtic thought also emphasized the symbolic numbers three, seven and twelve, but the triad dominated, expressing itself in the attributes of a god or a god-animal. The three-horned bull symbolized the power of virility and potency. What may be regarded as monstrosity is symbolic of supernatural power. The bull's head attached to a sceptre found at Willingham Fen (Cambs.) may be significant, but a bronze bull found at Maiden Castle has three females on its back, one of which seems to be a harpy linked with the underworld and death; another representing Diana is connected with childbirth and thus with the bringing of life. Shape-changing here assumes concrete form.

At Housesteads, three hooded figures gaze impassively at the spectator (17). The *Genii Cucullati*, identified by the *cucullus* or hooded cloak, were so well known that they could be sketched in outline on a relief from Cirencester.

17 *A relief depicting the* Genii Cucullati *from Housesteads, identified by their* cuculli *or hooded cloaks.*

As single figures they hold scrolls, moneybags, eggs as symbols of fertility, or are symbolic themselves having a phallic shape.

At Daglingworth (Glos.) they stand beside a mother goddess, the earth mother, who appears alone or in the power of the triad. Their cult, originating in northern Europe, became popular throughout the Roman world. Reliefs at Cirencester provide different interpretations. Stiff hierarchic figures, faces framed with braided hair, hold fruit, loaves and, in one case, a child, the ultimate symbol of fertility. A relief, carved by a sculptor trained in Classical form, depicts a relaxed happy group with toddlers playing between the mothers (**18**). As women in childbirth sought their protection, every detail has meaning, even the lapdog, a child's companion, but also symbolic of the underworld.

Cult of the head

A most powerful cult related to the severed head (**19**). The Celts hunted human heads as trophies, placing them on posts or hanging from trees. Posidonius (died *c.* 50 BC) commented that the Celts kept heads preserved in cedar-oil, a statement confirmed by pieces of skulls once preserved in oil found at Wroxeter, on what may be the site of a shrine. Livy remarked that,

18 *The cult of the mother goddesses originated in northern Europe but became popular throughout the Roman world. At Cirencester, Gloucestershire, their representations include a triad of women seated in a stern frontal pose holding loaves of bread, and, as shown on this relief, a relaxed group of mothers indulging their children. Both are intended to indicate a fertility cult.*

19 *Male head from York whose flowing locks recall the male Medusa head which forms the centre-piece of a shield on the pediment on the temple at Bath.*

34

decorated with gold and silver, heads were used as drinking cups. According to Strabo the Romans prohibited headhunting but the depiction of severed heads on Trajan's Column, erected in AD 113, suggests a custom permitted to auxiliaries in battle. The head had a life of its own. Singing heads and talking heads abound. In the *Mabinogion* (four tales of folk mythology compiled in the eleventh century, but relating to a much earlier tradition) Bran's severed head provided entertainment for his companions by singing and telling stories.

In Gaul, at the sacred sites of Roquepertuse and Entremont (near Aix en Provence in southern France), stone heads were carved alongside niches, where decapitated heads were displayed. Numerous stone heads found in Britain include one from Towcester (Northants), with staring eyes, carved on a block to allow it to stand freely. Sometimes the head served as an altar; one found at Corbridge had an indentation into which a libation could be poured. Horned heads are linked to Cernunnos, a horned deity associated with fertility, whose image glowers from such widely diverse objects as a bucket escutcheon at Aylesford (Kent) and a crudely carved block at Moresby (Cumbria). Heads are janiform: looking backwards to birth and forwards to death. The triad – three-faced or three-headed – silently watches all ways.

Bath

Complexity of function across cultures can be perceived at Bath, an important cult centre established in the first century AD. At the hot springs was worshipped the Celtic goddess Sulis, whom the Romans associated with Minerva, goddess of healing. A gilded bronze head, purely Classical in style and form, was probably part of her cult statue, but the carving on the temple pediment tells a different story. In the centre is a Gorgon's head derived from the breastplate of Minerva, which was designed to ward off evil; moustaches, which flow into the hair, identify it as male. Tongues of hair become sun-flames, the beard writhes with serpents: elements of water combine with elements of fire and earth. Yet Classical ele-

ments are present. Victories support the shield, and the owl, companion of Minerva, stands on a Corinthian helmet. This huge temple, set in the middle of a courtyard connected to the baths complex, was linked with a theatre, which also had a place in the healing process because laughter and drama can dissipate tension.

Classical temples were a feature of other important towns but actual remains are few. Excavations in the forum at Verulamium suggested that one temple of the three discovered there was in the Classical style. Possibly the temple at Chichester in West Sussex dedicated to Neptune and Minerva by the guild of ironworkers, was also built on Classical lines if only because the tribe of the Atrebates was responsive to Roman influence.

Romano-Celtic temples

Roman tolerance ensured that worshippers chose their own deity and offering and many would frequent the Romano-Celtic temples, so-called because they are found in the parts of the empire occupied by the Celts. Springhead in Kent with four temples seems to have been a pilgrimage centre, so was Uley (Glos.) where shelter was provided for visitors and officials of the cult. Most of these temples were tall, square buildings with small windows in the upper part and surrounded by a veranda; others were round or octagonal, some with a solid outer wall and an ambulatory inside. These might continue a pre-Roman religious site, possibly that of a sacred grove. Lucan, in the *Pharsalia*, written about AD 65, described such a grove in Gaul. The trees were smeared with human blood and idols of horrible aspect grinned out of the darkness, a literary reference to the cult of the human head. No bird or beast lived there, and, not surprisingly, all was silent. This place of terror is very different from a grove mentioned by Pliny the Elder, where mistletoe was collected with suitable reverence.

Shrines and votive gifts

Less elaborate places of worship existed. Coventina's shrine consisted of low walls set round a pool. Many wooden buildings, where offerings to deities were hung, have disappeared. Offerings included jewellery, pipeclay figurines, leaf-shaped plaques, bronze letters from which inscriptions could be made and small pots in which food and flowers were placed. Sometimes groups of figurines were presented. At Bruton, Somerset, figurines of Minerva and Mercury, found at the site, would have fitted neatly into a small shrine.

Offerings might be for services rendered; a pair of gold 'eyes', presented at Wroxeter, might be a thank-offering for a cure. But there could be a vicious element when requesting the god's aid. Curse tablets seeking vengeance on the perpetrators of a theft or an insult follow a certain formula because, like all such invocations, the form of words was vital. Their sonorous rhythm suggests the hand of a professional scribe. At Bath, Basilica demands the return of her silver ring crying that not only the person who has stolen it but anyone who knows anything about it or keeps silence may be cursed in (his/her) blood, eyes and every limb and have all intestines eaten away.

The supernatural was never far from the surface in religious belief. Amulets, needed to ward off evil, show the head of the Medusa on a cameo or pendant. A grave at Colchester contained a dog's tooth, a phallus and a bell together with a small model of a human head. The phallus was a powerful motif (20). Soldiers attached it to their horse-harness; men and women wore it as a pendant and, in London, a child was protected from an early age by having one engraved on a bezel set into a ring.

It is difficult to know where superstition ended and decoration began. Is an eight-rayed object found in a cache of jewellery intended for protection or decoration? Do wheels depict the Celtic sun wheel, the thunderbolt motif of the Roman Jupiter, a protection against evil, or a combination of all three? Do wheels buried in graves lighten the darkness, protect against the underworld, or are they merely a favourite piece of jewellery? Nothing, however, could be left to chance in a world where the rational was so closely interwoven with the supernatural.

20 *The phallus often acted as an amulet. This carving, found at Wroxeter, Shropshire, is a humorous depiction of a penis placed on wheels.*

Lararia

Figurines were placed on *lararia* (household shrines) on which the head of the household placed an offering, perhaps a libation of wine or a small cake. *Lararia* were often placed in the atrium (entrance hall), but Suetonius records that Domitian's murder in his bedchamber in AD 96 was witnessed by the boy attending to the shrine. *Lararia* took their name from the *lares,* originally gods of the fields and spirits of dead ancestors. The *lar familiaris*, god of the household accounts, was always worshipped in conjunction with the *penates,* the spirits of the household store cupboard.

Lares were always shown in pairs, having a dancing pose, and holding up a drinking horn in one hand and a wine vessel in the other to indicate the prosperity sought by the household. They were placed one on either side of a figurine of the *Genius Paterfamilias,* who represented the life spirit of both the master of the household and the reigning emperor (**21**). The toga placed over the head to ward off evil imitated the action which both took when sacrificing to the gods. Each man had his personal *Genius,* formed at birth and attached to him all his life. It was honoured on his birthday and, at his death, accompanied him to Hades. Some, like one from Brandon, Suffolk, hold cornucopias, symbols of plenty, which could also be held by the *lares.*

Christianity hastened the destruction of the shrines. A well at Lower Slaughter (Glos.) served as a receptacle for altars thrown in by wreckers, as

21 *Bronze figurines of a* lar familiaris *holding a double cornucopia, height 10.5cm (4.1in) from Brandon, Suffolk, and a* Genius Paterfamilias, *height 10.6cm (4.2in) from Richborough, Kent, which would once have been placed on household shrines.*

did Coventina's well. Gildas comments on the ruins of shrines, 'their walls inside and out bristling with idols of savage mien', and the Venerable Bede, writing in the eighth century, remarks that Roman temples could still be seen in his day, but many shrines had already fallen into decay, their purpose receding beyond memory.

Druids and priests

Roman toleration had its limits. Rome would not allow any challenge to her power and abhorred human sacrifice; on both counts she opposed Druidism. Tacitus records that when Suetonius Paulinus invaded Anglesey he cut down groves devoted to savage rites, where altars were drenched with the blood of human captives. Caesar's comment that those who wished to study Druidism more thoroughly went to Britain, implies that there Druidic custom was less diluted. The resistance in Anglesey suggests that Druids had established themselves in the less populated parts of the country.

The Druids were both priests and teachers. Caesar said that they officiated at worship, regulated public and private sacrifices and gave decisions on all religious questions. Their word was law; anyone disobeying was shunned by society. His information was probably obtained

37

first hand from Diviciacus, a Druid who combined the functions of priest and temporal ruler. There were also female Druids who acted as priestesses and seers; prophecies made to the emperors Alexander Severus, Diocletian and Aurelian in the third century were made by Druidesses.

Druids were not the only priests in Britain. Other Celtic priesthoods continued, providing that they did not oppose Rome, and official religion was organized on a priestly basis. Some priests were paid officials; others were recruited from the ranks of provincial or local officials and the native aristocracy. Elaborate priestly colleges were not necessary in Britain, but important temples such as at Bath would have needed some officials. C. Calpurnius Receptus describes himself on an altar as *sacerdos* of the goddess Sulis; L. Marcius Memor, a *haruspex*, who originated from North Italy, had probably been trained in his craft before he arrived at Bath.

Temples required slaves to clean the premises, servants to supervise ceremonies and oversee worshippers, and attendants to keep order and control access. Guards were needed to protect the equipment – *paterae* and flagons for pouring libations, bowls for washing priestly hands and sacrificial knives. Marcus Antonius Sabinus dedicated a bronze *patera* to Apollo Anextiomarus at South Shields, while Fabius Dubitatus spent handsomely to provide a silver *patera* with gold letters for the mother goddesses. This was found in a cache at Backworth, Tyne and Wear, and another cache from Thetford (Norfolk) had several silver spoons dedicated to the Roman woodland deity, Faunus.

Priests need regalia and vestments. At Hockwold-cum-Wilton in Norfolk one headdress is composed as a circular band with strips running up to cross over each other and a moulded point at the top. Small bronze plaques depicted severed heads, suggesting that the belief, if not the actual process, had been incorporated into the religious practice here.

An elaborate sceptre from Willingham Fen has a nude deity with his foot placed on a grotesque figure, a clear reference to the cult of Jupiter Taranis. A wheel, an eagle, a dolphin and a three-horned bull are references to other cults. Other sceptres had busts of deities on the top, Jupiter from Amersham (Bucks.) and Mars from Brough-on-Humber, Humberside. A fine bronze head from Worlington (Cambs.) portrays Hadrian. These sceptres continued an Iron Age custom, where human-headed sceptres replaced the tradition of carrying human heads on poles.

Ritual

The priests supervised religious rites, but temples were not intended for congregational worship. They housed cult statues of deities and provided a repository for offerings. Worshippers placed incense or poured a libation on the altar to make a contract: if the deity granted a request then homage would be paid to that god. The worshipper might light a lamp and would be expected to provide money towards the upkeep of the building or the cost of a sacrifice.

Public worship could take the form of a procession, accompanied by music played on pipes, cymbals, rattles and tambourines. This ended in a sacrifice, performed on the altar in the courtyard in front of the temple. Every action was checked and regulated. Juvenal (died *c.* AD 130) speaks of the animal tugging at its rope to hurry to the sacrifice; if it held back it would be an inauspicious start.

A scene on the right side of a distance-slab on the Antonine Wall at Bridgeness gives an equally vivid picture of a sacrifice (**22**). The impression is not one of a quiet ceremony. A servant plays the double pipe, while a ram, a boar and a bull are not waiting patiently to be sacrificed but are adding their cries to the noise. The chief celebrant is still making his libation over the altar but already one priest crouches with the knife waiting for the moment of action. As there are three animals, they would be pole-axed before being killed. The *suovetaurilia,* or sacrifice, is being made by the Second Legion Augusta but it represents a scene which could have been enacted on the altar at Bath, at Colchester, or any other temple in Britain.

22 *One of the distance-slabs from Bridgeness, West Lothian, gives a vivid picture of the* suovetaurilia, *or sacrifice, commemorating the beginning or ending of a great task, in this case the building of the Antonine Wall.*

Mithras

The official cults of Rome did not excite emotion in their devotees, hence the popularity of cults from the eastern parts of the empire. Mithras, a Persian god, was important to soldiers because he represented the victory of the soul after death, and to merchants as the god of fair trading. As an offshoot of Zoroastrianism, this sophisticated cult appealed to intellectuals, especially in the second and third centuries, when men were seeking to understand the world of the cosmos.

At Rudchester, Mithras is represented as born springing from a rock, but at Housesteads he emerges from the cosmic egg, symbol of resurrection. The egg-shaped frame depicts the signs of the zodiac; lamps placed behind the sculpture would surround Mithras with awe-inspiring light, an effect deliberately conflating him, as inscribed on another altar, with the Invincible Sun. Another startling effect was intended at Carrawburgh, where a male solar deity wears a crown, its rays pierced to let light shine through.

Mithras was worshipped in a Mithraeum, often built partly underground with side benches on which worshippers reclined to feast; chicken was especially popular, judging by the bones found in the London Mithraeum. At the end of the building was the tauroctony, the slaying of the wild bull. From the body sprang plants useful to man, from the blood came the vine of life, and from the spinal cord and the tail came wheat. Thus death and creation are one. A dog and a serpent, symbolizing the underworld, lap the blood, while a scorpion tries to prevent the act of creation.

At Housesteads and Carrawburgh were found the companions of Mithras: *Cautes,* whose upturned torch indicated life and light, and *Cautopates,* casting his torch downwards to signify darkness and death. As Mithraism was practised in secrecy many of the details are obscure but, according to St Jerome, writing in the fourth/fifth centuries, devotees had to pass through seven grades. For some of these special dress was worn; men wearing heads of ravens and lions are depicted on reliefs.

Progression to each grade was by tests, including ordeals of fire and water. Some were symbolic: hands were covered in honey, which countered evil. Others were more unpleasant. To the left of the entrance to the Carrawburgh Mithraeum was a pit, which, when covered with stones on which a fire might be lit, would give any man suffering from claustrophobia a terrifying experience. On a silver box found in the London Mithraeum a man symbolically saved from death emerges from such a tomb. The box contained an infuser, possibly for straining wine, but more likely for herbs. Incense, giving a soporific effect, could be placed in a burner found at Rudchester, and pine-cones found at Carrawburgh would produce a pleasant smell when burned.

In the fourth century many of the ceremonies, including a sacred meal (which initiates believed

23 *A statue of the goddess Juno Regina, consort of Jupiter Dolichenus, standing on a heifer. The goddess, worshipped by women in childbirth, wears a long tunic and a stole with an embroidered edge.*

was indicative of a better life beyond this world), the ritual use of wine and water, and the celebration of 25 December as the birthday of Mithras, roused the wrath of the Christians. Violent attacks on Mithraea in Britain may have been initiated by the visit of the Emperor Constantine in AD 312. Mithras' followers buried objects and altars to save them, but sculptures were smashed by impious hands. Members of the Caernarfon Mithraeum (Gwynedd) dismantled it, but long after this the remains were deliberately destroyed as if to profane the site for ever.

Cybele and Atys

Other eastern cults included that of Jupiter Dolichenus and his consort Juno Regina (**23**). But more popular was the cult of Cybele, whose worship had been accepted into the State religion in Rome in the third century BC. Her companion, Atys, appears with his symbolic Phrygian cap – a pointed cap turned forward at the front – on an altar from Gloucester where he plays pipes to indicate the joyous nature of Cybele's festival. His presence on sepulchral monuments at York, Chester and Caerleon is to reassure her followers of their rebirth in the next world.

Figures wearing a Phrygian cap found in London hint at a temple but there is more conclusive evidence. Both Atys and Cybele appear as bronze heads, together with those of other deities, on a pair of bronze forceps found in the Thames, thrown into the river either as a votive offering or to save it from Christians. Aspiring priests and worshippers, working themselves to a frenzy on Cybele's natal day, 24 March, castrated themselves in devotion to her service. The forceps staunched the blood. The act imitates Atys castrating himself as an act of retribution for a moment of infidelity towards the goddess. After his mutilation, he died and was resurrected, which explains Christian hostility.

The ceremony included slaying a bull over a pit to drench his followers in the reviving blood. A temple discovered at York, believed to be dedicated to Atys, had six skulls in the floor, possibly from the sacrificed bulls. As Atys was a hunting god, the hunting scene on a beaker also buried in the floor may be significant. The temple, erected in AD 180 and in use for over 200 years, was part of a religious complex situated in the civil district on the main road leading south of the *colonia*.

Egyptian deities

Egypt also contributed to Roman religious life. Isis (**24**), who gave birth to Harpocrates, was connected with the numerous mother goddess cults. Her husband, Osiris, was killed and dismembered by Seth. Isis restored Osiris to life and gave Harpocrates the task of avenging his father. The myth yet again embraces the essential elements of birth, death and resurrection so that it attracted converts from the intellectual strata of society. One such was M. Martiannius Pulcher, provincial governor stationed in London in the third century, who ordered a temple of Isis to be restored; according to an inscription reused in the riverside wall, it had collapsed due to old age. As protectress in childbirth, Isis was worshipped by women; others were attracted by the mystic nature of the cult, the chanting of priests and the intoning of seven vowels.

Isis' consort, Osiris, was linked with the Greco-Roman Serapis, whose fertility connection was indicated by a corn modius (corn measure) on his head. One such head was found in the London Mithraeum and another at Silchester. The god had a temple at York built in the second century on the order of the legate of the Sixth Legion, Claudius Hieronymianus, whose name betrays his Near Eastern origins (**25**).

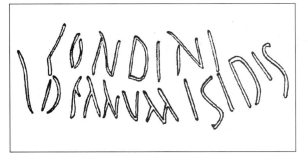

24 *An inscription on a jug found in London reads* Londinium ad fanum Isis *(London, at the temple of Isis). The jug may have been part of the temple plate or have been used in an establishment nearby.*

25 *An inscription found at York records the building of a temple to Serapis by Claudius Hieronymianus, legate of the Sixth Legion Victrix, who may have been governor of Cappadocia at the end of the second century AD.*

Bacchus

A more riotous god was Bacchus, whose popularity is attested as much in works of art as in religion. He was a saviour god, who in Greek mythology rescued Ariadne when she was abandoned by Theseus on the island of Naxos, but he also has eastern connections and as such he rides a tiger, or, as a mosaic in London interprets, a panther. He was a dangerous god because his association with wine made his followers tipsy (**26**).

Christianity

Christianity could be considered as an oriental cult but with one essential difference: Christian belief might lead to persecution but ensured everlasting life. The Romans believed this was merely another mystery cult. Jesus had lived in Judea, converted men and women to his 'cult', been crucified, died, buried and after three days – one of the mystic numbers – had been resurrected. He also instructed his followers to eat his body and drink his blood. Christ was the son of God and, through him, a father God had been revealed to the chosen flock. This God was ruler and thus *Invictus* or 'Unconquered'. This linked both God and Christ to the sun and it is this aspect which is portrayed on a large mosaic found at Hinton St Mary, where the chi-rho monogram (the first two letters of the name of Christ in Greek) forms the

41

26 *A marble statuette of Bacchic revelry found in the Mithraeum in London. The god reels unsteadily, clutching at a serpent crawling along the overhead vines. Accompanying him are his carousing companions, a satyr, Silenus and a maenad. On the upper left can be seen the legs of Pan, who would have been perched on the branches of the vines.*

pattern of the sun's rays behind the head of the God–Christ (**27**).

The term *Invictus* applied to Mithras, and to Hercules, who had gone to Hades and returned just as Christ had returned to life. Thus Christianity, according to the Romans, was not

27 *Mosaic from the Hinton St Mary villa, Dorset, depicting the head of Christ. Behind is the chi-rho monogram.*

the sole cult for humankind but one of many which Roman tolerance embraced. The owner of the Hinton St Mary mosaic need not have been Christian, but like many others been desirous of expanding his knowledge. Another mosaic found in the same villa, and still *in situ*, takes the theme of Bellerophon mounted on a Pegasus slaying the Chimaera, a victory of good over evil, whose death also brings forth life. This also appears on a pavement in the Lullingstone villa in Kent (see **75**), where the owner turned one room into a Christian church, so that members could enter from the outside. These mosaics indicate belief displayed in allegorical form; the Orpheus pavements, so popular in the south-west, may be a reference to Christ as the Good Shepherd, protector of animals and men.

Christ's followers, however, were expected to follow a moral code and to partake of the central mystery unfolded by Christ in the Last Supper. This meal, and the ritual attached to it, needed sacred vessels, such as those discovered in a buried hoard at Water Newton composed of silver bowls, cups, spoons, flagons and wine stoups. The majority of the twenty-eight silver items bear the Christian monogram or have inscriptions which can be interpreted in a Christian fashion. Decoration and motifs found on spoons and other objects in other hoards, like that discovered at Thetford, may indicate that for some people belief in Christianity and pagan cults fused.

The chi-rho (**28**) does presuppose some link with Christian belief. Placed within a circle, however, as on one of the Water Newton plaques, thus conflating the wheel and the solar cults, it

43

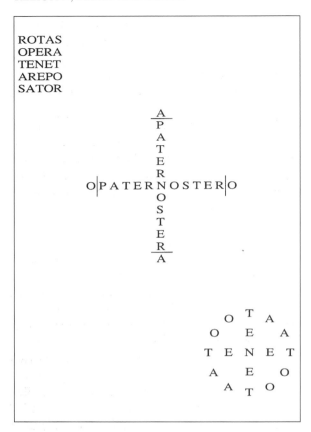

```
ROTAS
OPERA
TENET
AREPO
SATOR
                        A
                        P
                        A
                        T
                        E
                        R
              O|P A T E R N O S T E R|O
                        O
                        S
                        T
                        E
                        R
                        A


                          O     T     A
                        O     E     A
                        T  E  N  E  T
                        A     E     O
                          A     T  O
```

28 *The Christian word-game found sketched on a piece of wallplaster at Cirencester and on a potsherd at Manchester could be interpreted as a magical acrostic which a Christian could adapt, rather than an indication of a belief in Christ.*

has links with Celtic religion. Devotees of Celtic cults may have been more easily brought to Christianity because of this.

The chi-rho also had political affiliations. In the early fourth century Christianity had been adopted as the State religion by the Emperor Constantine, who believed that a vision of that symbol at the battle of the Milvian Bridge ensured him victory and thus the empire. The chi-rho appeared on coins issued by the House of Constantine and those of later emperors, large numbers of which have been found in deposits in Britain. The monogram appeared on the ends of coffins and, surrounded by a wreath as at Lullingstone, decorated the wall of a house chapel. It has been found scratched on walls at Cirencester and Manchester.

On the administrative side the evidence is more positive. By the early fourth century Britain had at least three bishops, who are reported as attending the Council of Arles in AD 314, so poor that they had to have monetary support. Bishops suggest an organized Church but this organization had been hard won. Other religions had no difficulty in accepting the concept of a divine emperor and worship of his divinity. This Christians could not accept, nor could they peacefully coexist with belief which refused to acknowledge one true God. Refusal to worship the emperor was treason to the State, so that Christians were persecuted as much for political reasons as for religious ones.

Martyrs were inevitable. Aaron, whose name suggests a convert from Judaism, and Julius met their deaths in the Caerleon amphitheatre; Alban was martyred at Verulamium, where a city and a cathedral were to bear his name. Christianity bred resentment and, even when adopted as the State religion, its intolerance infuriated those who wished to worship the old gods. It was also accused of preaching resignation to an intolerable existence. Yet Christianity could offer hope of a better life in the next world, providing that earthly life was lived according to a moral code. Accordingly it began to make converts.

Christians need not have wished to advertise their faith but there might be a doubt about their intentions. An inhabitant of the Chedworth villa (Glos.) might idly scratch the chi-rho symbol on a stone, as would a citizen of York on a tile or a citizen of Leicester on a brick. Does this imply faith or were they trying out a newfangled piece of graffito? The Christian faith still had to compete with pagan gods, with their hold on those who lived so close to nature. That persistence of devotion to natural phenomena can be noted, when Canon 23 of the second Council of Arles in AD 452 ordered bishops to prevent the heathen from venerating trees, fountains and stones. In the seventh century the homilies of St Eloi, Bishop of Noyon, urged trust in the mercy of God and not in trees, fountains or crossroads, and the Councils of Rouen and Toledo denounced stone worship.

Britain had difficulty in abandoning the old gods. Bede recounts that when St Augustine arrived in Britain in AD 597 he met King Ethelbert of Kent in the open air as the king feared that Augustine might practise magic in the confines of his house. Pope Gregory the Great in AD 601 advised Abbot Miletus, whom he was sending to Britain, that temple idols were to be destroyed but not the buildings, 'for if those temples are well-built, it is requisite that they be converted from the worship of devils to the worship of the true God'. God would be worshipped in the places where pagans had been accustomed to gather. It is clear that in Britain, as elsewhere, the struggle of Christianity for the minds of men and women was to continue long after the Roman era.

The disposal of the dead: Celtic practice

'Death comes at last and lays cold hands upon me.' To Celtic heroes death was welcomed as the entry into the otherworld, a place of feasting and fighting. According to Irish mythology, there were five banqueting halls forming a Celtic Valhalla, each having a cauldron, which gave everyone his proper food in an inexhaustible supply. Many graves contain food or a beaker of drink, enough to tide the person over the journey. This ritual occurred even when the dead had to be buried hastily, as when the Roman forces attacked the hill-fort of Maiden Castle. During a lull in the fighting shallow graves were hastily dug and the people buried with the necessary provisions. Complete pig skeletons have been found at Snailwell (Cambs.), and in Irish mythology the pig was so characteristic of the otherworld that the lord of the feast was sometimes represented as a man carrying a pig.

A richly furnished grave at Baldock (Herts.) contained amphorae, a cauldron, pottery and bronze vessels; two pairs of fire-dogs provided separate hearth furniture for the deceased and a guest. A bone flute at Stanfordbury (Beds.) hinted that entertainment was expected. Many items found in graves had been smashed or bent, either to 'kill' them, so that the deceased took

with him in spirit what he could not take in person, or to forestall tomb robbers. This form of burial continued into Roman Britain. At Holborough (Kent) the grave contained five smashed amphorae, over which a libation of wine had been poured.

Cremation cemeteries have been found at Aylesford and Swarling, Kent. There are few inhumation cemeteries. Probably excarnation, the exposing of bodies until the flesh had rotted, took place. The bones would be collected together to be used for ritual purposes.

Roman funerary belief

In Roman Britain burial was carefully regulated. The law of the Twelve Tables, first promulgated during the republic, forbade burial within the walls of a town, so that the dead did not pollute either physically or spiritually the material world. At Housesteads two burials under the floor of a house aroused the excavators' suspicions that here was a double murder. The ruling did not apply to children who were stillborn or died under ten days old, because they were regarded as having no legal existence. Cemeteries placed outside a town, often alongside main roads, defined the boundaries of the towns as well as making it easier to carry out rituals attending the dead.

Examination of the cemeteries at York evokes strong suspicion that the dead were as divided in death as they were in life. The Trentholme Drive cemetery, which lay quite far away from the town, seems to have been a burial place for the poorer classes; there were fewer coffins and grave-goods, and burials were made without caring about previous ones (**29**). Closer to the town, graves were marked by tiled graves (**30**) or handsome stone reliefs, while burials just outside the walls were placed in stone coffins and covered with gypsum, possibly to preserve the bodies for the afterlife as well as preventing tomb-robbing.

Roman funerary belief postulated this afterlife, but it was a more shadowy place than the Celtic afterlife, although with the suggestion of a good life rewarded and evil-doers punished. Roman

29 *Skeletons excavated in graves in the Trentholme Drive cemetery, York.*

funerary practice entailed both ritual which accompanied the disposal of the body, and rites to ensure that the spirit stayed in the next world and did not return to haunt the living. Sometimes the body was placed face downwards or beheaded after death, with the head placed by the side of the legs or at the feet to prevent the dead from returning. On the whole, until the second century AD, cremation was the normal practice, but gradually inhumation became the custom. This is exemplified at Dorchester-on-Thames (Oxon.), where cremation was practised until the 180s, to be followed by cremation and inhumation together, and from about AD 280 inhumation alone. But there seem to have been areas where cremations continued: the fourth-century cemetery at Lankhills, Winchester, contained only cremations.

When a person died the closest relative closed the eyes and began a formal lament while the body was washed and anointed. A man would be dressed in a toga, a woman in a long tunic. In Rome there would be no difficulty in obtaining a toga but in Britain this might be more rare. Fragments of material found in graves suggest more a woollen shroud than a formal garment. There were exceptions. At Holborough a dead child seems to have been draped in a rich purple cloth. Hob-nails found in coffins suggest that the deceased were shod for the walk to the afterlife.

Funerary processions were held at night. The deceased, carried on a funerary bed, preceded by musicians and followed by grieving mourners,

30 *A tiled grave found in York.*

31 *A funerary procession as portrayed on a tomb at Rome. The deceased, accompanied by his grieving widow and children and professional mourners, is being carried on a litter. Music is provided by musicians playing double pipes; the leading man plays the* lituus *or long trumpet, those following play the* cornu, *a long curved tube, tuned to a G with a range of seventeen notes and with a tone like a French horn.*

was carried to the cemetery where a funerary oration was declaimed over the body (**31**). At Trentholme Drive, York, piles of ashes and a burnt area reveal the cremation place. Reverently collected, the ashes would be placed in a glass or pottery container.

The deceased had a journey to make, in particular to cross the Styx in Charon's boat. To pay him a coin was needed, often placed in the mouth for safekeeping. Coins found at York indicate that one was included even in the case of cremations. At Roden Down, Compton (Berks.), seven of ten people had their payment ready; but at Rams Hill, also in Berkshire, the coin edges were sharp as if they had been clipped. Someone was prepared to take the risk of cheating Charon.

Charcoal placed in the grave is a symbol of change, while lamps provide light for the dead and make them feel at home. At York one person insisted on having an elaborate candelabra. Miniature objects – an iron shovel at Luton, near Chatham in Kent, and shovel and tongs at Litlington (Cambs.) – represented the real tools. Phials and small bottles once contained perfume; frankincense was suspected in one grave at Weston Turville (Bucks.). Women took their favourite jewellery, or tweezers and other toilet articles to beautify themselves after death. Brooches once fastened shrouds; men had knives and tools. At Winchester a shale trencher was placed carefully by the side of a cremation; on it were eating implements together with half a pig's skull and a leg of pork with close by a drinking vessel: refreshment for the last journey.

Relatives had further obligations. Ceremonies took place on anniversaries to ensure that the dead were remembered. Those who had no relatives, a soldier or a slave, had these duties performed by a guild. The mausoleum was opened so that a meal could be put in, or, as at Caerleon and Chichester, the dead were nourished by pouring liquid through the neck of an amphora or a pipe. For poorer people these also served as a grave-marker.

Funerary banquets

The funerary banquet seems to suggest a tradition of survival of the dead person's spirit as well as an intimation of everlasting life, although there may be a contradiction here: the death of the body released the spirit yet the feeding of a dead body implies some kind of life spirit is still present within the skeletal form. The Fathers of the Church preached against this practice, which lasted a long time. Burchard, Bishop of Worms, warned in as late as the eleventh century against eating anything offered to idols, especially offerings made at the tombs of the dead. Eggs found at Colchester and York may be part of the funerary feast or represent the symbol of regeneration.

A funerary banquet appears pictorially in the iconography of the tombstone. At Chester and York the deceased is shown resting on a funerary bed. Curatia Dinysia at Chester holds up a cup as a reminder of what she is missing in life; Julia

Velva at York has her cup placed on a small table. Pine-cones in the spandrels symbolize mourning and felicity; dolphins and tritons – the journey; poppies – sleep and death; rosettes and stars – prosperity and apotheosis in the next world, and lions – devouring death (**32**). Tombstones depict the full panoply and iconography of mourning; sometimes, as at Colchester where a sphinx holds a human head between its paws, Celtic and Roman funerary belief merges.

Tombstones

Tombstone inscriptions observed a fairly conventional pattern. *Dis manibus* (to the spirits of the departed-world) was followed by the person's name and age. An official or soldier might include details of his rank, status and career. The names of the person who erected the stone – a freedman,

the heir or a sorrowing wife – were sometimes added. Inscriptions are poignant. At Bath, Vettius Romulus and Victoria Sabina wept for their dearest daughter who lived three years, four months and nine days, while at York Felicius Simplex mourned his daughter, Simplicia Florentina, 'a most innocent soul', who lived ten months.

Some are precisely detailed. Lucius Vitellius Tancinus, son of Mantaius, a tribesman of Caurium in Spain, trooper of the cavalry regiment of Vettones, Roman citizen, had 26 years of service before he died at Bath aged 46, possibly while he was trying to regain his health. Some reliefs are stereotyped. Tombstones at Cirencester and Gloucester depicting cavalrymen riding over a prostrate enemy have their origins in Gaul and the Rhineland. On the tombstone at Chester of one unfortunate *optio*, whose career was cut short when he was lost at sea off the Cheshire coast while awaiting promotion to centurion, the doors of death carved on the tomb are merely symbolic (**33**).

32 *Funerary heads carved in the Celtic style found at Burrow Heights, Lancaster, which may have decorated a tomb.*

33 *The tombstone of an* optio *lost in a shipwreck off the coast of Cheshire. The letters H S E are abbreviations for* Hic Situs Est *(Here he lies) but the H has been omitted presumably because the body was never found.*

Coffins and other burials

Wealthy people were buried in stone or lead sarcophagi and at York liquid gypsum was poured into coffins. There are no elaborate stone coffins such as were found elsewhere in the empire, but Caecilius Rufus buried his 27-year-old wife, Aelia Severa, in a handsomely lettered coffin at York. Later, however, she was unceremoniously bundled out in order that an unknown man, covered with gypsum, might be buried in the coffin; the family tombstone for Flavia Augustina was used as a lid. There was no feeling that the dead should be left undisturbed in perpetuity. At both York and Chester in the late third century funerary reliefs were dug up and used in the construction of the defences. Eventually the central authority forbade such desecration.

Elsewhere, mausolea might indicate wealth or family groupings, like the one at Lullingstone. Several persons placed in mausolea at Poundbury, Dorchester, had gypsum burials. A prominent way of marking a grave was to build a steep-sided barrow over it as in the groups at Bartlow (Cambs.) and the so-called Six Hills at Stevenage (Herts.). Not all burials would be as prominent as these, and not everyone would wish to be buried according to Roman rites. Certainly Celtic practices continued. Christianity also affected burial practice; grave-goods became less frequent and bodies were placed with their heads to the west.

But death, no matter how it came, was keenly felt and whatever burial custom was followed grief was there. Occasionally the poignancy comes through the centuries. An inscription on a tombstone at Lincoln laments a 'sweetest child' aged nine, using words similar to those which Virgil uses in the sixth book of the *Aeneid* that she had been 'torn away no less suddenly than the partner of Dis', a despairing cry of a life brought to an untimely end. And the wistful words of Titus Flaminius at Wroxeter recall a life richly lived, 'the gods prohibit you from the winegrape and water when you enter Tartarus'.

3
Recreation, leisure and public entertainment

The term 'leisure' means more than mere abstention from work. It implies time used for relaxation, allowing recuperation from daily pressures; it can be diversion as an antidote to boredom or an opportunity to broaden knowledge, encouraging the development of personality and an implication that people need to improve themselves, morally as well as physically.

All these might be found in Romano-British society, but the time available for leisure activities would depend on a person's social status and geographical locality. For many people, especially those at subsistence level, only the first two definitions would apply. The only relaxation from a hard-working life would be time spent in sleep or an exhausted pause between essential tasks; even enforced leisure because of bad weather might be welcomed. In towns there would be opportunity both for diverting entertainments and for the broadening of knowledge and personality. Roman society also utilized leisure time more cynically by providing entertainment for the masses in a successful bid to buy their support.

Story-telling

An enjoyable way of utilizing leisure time, and one common in the pre-Roman Iron Age, was the telling of tales. The itinerant story-teller relating the sagas of Celtic heroes would be welcomed. Many of these were retold until they were written down several centuries after they were first devised in non-literate form. The two great tales of Irish Celtic literature – the Ulster cycle of Cu Chulainn and the Southern Irish adventures of Finn Mac Cumaill – together with the Welsh epic of the *Mabinogion,* owe their survival to oral tradition before they were committed to writing during the Christian era.

Mention has already been made of the Celtic capacity for memorizing verses. Athenaeus, quoting Posidonius in the third century AD, says that the Celts have entertainers, whom they call bards, 'poets delivering eulogies in song'. Strabo criticizes their childish boastfulness, but Posidonius' account is confirmed by Diodorus Siculus in the first century BC, who comments that bards 'sing to the accompaniment of instruments like lyres either in praise of people or to deride them'. This derision was the satirizing of an enemy, where the vehemence of oral onslaught could mentally paralyse a man. The love of words was effective in the devising of riddles, the hidden shape-changing of meaning, which disguises the true intention.

The tendency to exaggerate and boast was second nature to the story-tellers, as was the rhythmical nature of description, allied with vivid, picturesque language. In the *Mabinogion,* Culhwch makes his way to the court of the king riding in a chariot, 'with two greyhounds, white-breasted, brindled, in front of him, with a collar of red gold about the neck of either, from shoulder swell to ear, the one that would be on the left side would be on the right, and the one that was on the right side would be on the left, like sea swallows sporting round him'. The same story contains lengthy repetition of the conditions set out by the giant Ysbaddaden, when Culhwch sought the hand of his daughter.

In Roman Britain groups sitting in the firelight of a roundhouse on a winter's evening, or outside in the heat of the summer, would hear tales of their mythological ancestors. Such tales could have been told as a curious, diverting amusement at a dinner party held in London, Silchester or Verulamium. But in the houses of those eager to express their adherence to Rome, or others brought up on such stories, might be recounted tales from Roman history or mythology. In the Low Ham villa a story-teller might use the illustrations on the handsome mosaic to retell the story of Dido and Aeneas.

Music

Leisure activities at home included making music. Irish literature reveals that the Celts were excellent harpists and Diodorus' words indicate that they had no difficulty in accompanying themselves on the lyre. The technique is somewhat similar for both instruments but the Romans introduced the cithara, where the strings worked in conjunction with a soundbox and were stroked or plucked with a plectrum. Dedicated performers were reported to have made remarkable music from them. This instrument may be that played by Orpheus as he charms the animals on the mosaic pavements from Dyer Court and Barton Farm, Cirencester.

Pipes are mentioned in both Celtic and Latin texts. It would be surprising if this musical talent was lost to the Celts especially as the Romans enjoyed making music. Several bone flutes have been found in Britain and part of a wooden reed-pipe came from a well at Ashton (Northants). A set of pan-pipes, called a syrinx, made of boxwood, and with notes of B flat, C, D, E and G, was found in London near Southwark Bridge. The mosaic now in Sherborne Castle showing

34 A mosaic depicting the musical contest between Apollo playing the lyre and Marsyas playing the double pipes. Although on the mosaic Marsyas appears to be dancing in triumph, he lost the contest and was flayed alive for his presumption; from his blood flowed a river which bears his name.

35 *A bronze figurine of a female pipe-player from Silchester, Hampshire.*

the contest between Apollo and Marsyas depicts the former playing the lyre and the latter the double pipes (**34**). A bronze figurine found at Silchester shows a young girl waiting to play what appears to be a tibia, which issued a drone-like note (**35**).

Musical entertainment was particularly appreciated during feasts and dinner parties. Items were interspersed with songs, poetry, readings from historians and, no doubt, telling of heroic tales. Four terracotta reclining diners found in a child's grave at Colchester seem to be listening to readings given by reciters who hold scrolls on trays in front of them. Athletes could be brought in to perform gymnastics. The small bronze figure found in the Thames near London Bridge adjusts his hair casually while waiting to throw a weight. Possibly the girl who disposed of a torn bikini down a first-century well in London might also have raised applause by her acrobatics.

A birthday party

Women could be present at dinner parties although surely not all arrived in the state indicated by Juvenal, who writes of one woman arriving late for dinner 'with thirst enough to drink off the vessel containing full three gallons which is laid at her feet and from which she tosses off a couple of pints before dinner to create a raging appetite; then she brings it all up again and souses the floor with the washings of her insides'.

A unique piece of evidence from Vindolanda comes from a writing tablet on which was written an invitation to a birthday party to which Claudia Severa invites her friend or relative, Sulpicia Lepidina, wife of Flavius Cerialis, prefect of the Ninth Cohort of Batavians, stationed at Vindolanda at the end of the first century. Claudia lived at a fort commanded by her husband, Aelius Brocchus, called *Briga,* probably Kirkbride, near Carlisle. A military escort would have to be provided to escort Sulpicia across thirty-five miles of rough country in order as Claudia says 'to make the day more enjoyable by your presence'. The letter seems to have been written by a professional scriptwriter but to make sure that Sulpicia came on that special day, the third day before the Ides of September (10 September). sometime in the year AD 100, Claudia added in her own hand, 'I will expect you sister. Farewell sister, my dearest soul as I hope to prosper, and greetings.'

Children's play and ball games

Children could be kept quiet with clay or wooden dolls. The terracotta figures at Colchester may be part of a children's play-set. Small animals, suggested to have a ritual meaning, could be children's toys, like the carved jet bears found at Malton in North Yorkshire, Colchester and York. The parents of a little boy buried at York sent him to the otherworld with his bronze mouse as companion. Model dogs are a reminder that children have always wanted a cat or a dog as a pet, and we can imagine the glee with which children watched both cat and dog leaving their paw prints on wet tiles at the Lullingstone villa. On tombstones at York, Julia Velva's daughter and six-year-old Sempronia Martina both cradle birds in their hands. The unknown mother on a tombstone at Murrill Hill (Cumbria) allows her child to gently caress her bird.

Little children at Corbridge and York are shown holding balls on their tombstones. Balls were juggled and were used in a game called *trigon,* where three players threw balls between them. Galen, the Greek philosopher and physician of the second century AD, approved of ball games, because they needed quick movements and provided moderate exercise. One of the oldest ball games is 'kingy', where the ball is thrown at someone who has to hit it away with a bat or a hand; if hit elsewhere, he or she becomes the target. Balls were made of hair and an ox or pig's bladder. A figure holding a curved stick and clutching a ball can also be seen on a pottery mould from Kettering (Northants).

The Celts were dextrous at juggling. Cu Chulainn played his way to the court of his uncle, King Conchobar, by hitting a ball with a bronze curved stick, throwing the stick after it, then a javelin and lastly a spear. Rushing after them he would catch them in sequence, delicately holding the spear by its slender tip. When he arrived at the court he found the boy pages playing a ball game similar to hurling and, needless to say, in true heroic fashion he stops thrice fifty balls from going into a hole and puts thrice fifty balls in it. When Sidonius Apollinaris, Bishop of Clermont in the fifth century, visited a friend's house in Nîmes, he noticed on one side of the portico teams of ball-players throwing and catching balls with swift turns and agile ducking; on the other were groups of gamblers dicing.

Board games

Gambling and board games were very popular. Bone dice with similar markings as today have been found in civilian (York, London, Silchester) and military (Richborough, Newstead) contexts; at York, jet carvers took pride in working dice in that material. A dice-box has been found in London. Gaming pieces made of glass, pottery and bone are common (**colour plate 4**); bone ones at York were lathe-turned to give a flat surface. Some from Leicester had such worn edges that it was suggested that they had been used for playing tiddly-winks; closer examination indicated that they had been made from long bones which made it impossible to obtain a totally flat surface. In Silchester pieces were made of shale brought from Dorset, possibly from scrap left over from furniture-making, and some ingenious craftsman had drilled counters out of the shoulder-blade of a sheep.

Although boards of gold and silver, like those mentioned in the *Mabinogion,* may have been present in Britain, none has been found. More usual were boards scratched on tiles like the one found at Silchester and on stone blocks as at Richborough and Corbridge. At the Chedworth villa it would seem that one of the best places for playing a board game was on squares scratched on to a well-head. These boards might be for playing the game of *ludus latrunculorum,* the 'soldiers', where the board is marked out in eight by eight squares (or seven by seven at Silchester). This game is a kind of chess, where one piece is taken by being trapped by two enemy pieces. Forward and backward moves were allowed and the game was won by the player capturing the majority of the opponent's pieces.

We are uncertain of the precise rules of *brandub* and *fidchell* mentioned in the Irish epic of the *Táin Bó Cuailnge,* but we do know what game was played by soldiers at Holt, the works depot for Chester. The gaming board found there has a distinct pattern of two outer rows of ivy leaves separated into groups of six by a geometrical pattern surrounded by a circle (**36**). Another row in the centre consists of six pairs of scrolls with a

36 *A gaming board found at Holt (Clwyd) was used by soldiers of the Twentieth Legion to play the Roman game of* ludus duodecim scriptorum.

similar geometrical pattern in the middle. On this board, soldiers of the Twentieth Legion played *ludus duodecim scriptorum*, the game of twelve lines, a kind of backgammon. The players used three dice and the highest throws were the sixes. Sometimes letters were used instead of symbols or numbers. One known in Rome read:

LEVATE DALOCU	Jump up, push off,
LUDERE NESCIS	you don't know how to play,
IDIOTA REDECE	get out, stupid.

Great passions could be aroused by this game. Paintings found at Pompeii show players being forcefully ejected by a bouncer shouting, 'Get out if you want to fight.' Gambling games had been forbidden in the late republic, except during Saturnalia, but during the empire such prohibitions were completely disregarded.

A poignant memory of a love of gaming was found at the Lullingstone villa. About AD 300 a young man aged about twenty-four, and possibly the heir to the estate, was interred in a spacious mausoleum. A double tragedy is hinted at as a young woman was interred close by.

Accompanying the bodies were bottles and flagons, which once held drinks, and knives for cutting up meat in the otherworld. On his coffin were the remains of what appeared to be a folded, wooden gaming board and thirty glass gaming pieces, fifteen red and fifteen white, together with a bone disc on which had been scratched the head of Medusa, who would ward off evil. Here, in the cold gloom of the mausoleum, two young people had been provided with the means of playing an endless game of *ludus duodecim scriptorum* among the shades of the otherworld.

Hunting

Hunting on horseback, but more often on foot, could be classified both as work – necessary for the provision of food – and as a leisure pursuit. The Celtic passion for hunting often appears in the Irish and Welsh texts, where there is equal respect for hunted as well as hunter. Stories of boar, deer and bird hunting are told with great gusto, in particular the hunting of the great boar Twrch Trwyth in the *Mabinogion* and the legendary boar of Formael in the Irish Fenian cycle – grey, horrible, without ears, without tail . . . teeth standing out long and horrid outside his head – who in one day killed fifty hounds and fifty warriors.

The Romans, whose love of hunting as sport and exercise equalled that of the Celts, had ample opportunities in a country as wild as Britain, which had not been denuded of animals as had occurred in other areas of the empire. Some animals were captured, if Martial's words on the appearance of the Caledonian bear in the amphitheatres of Rome indicate reality and not poetic licence.

Strabo noted that Celtic Britain exported dogs 'bred specifically for hunting'. The Romans were able to take advantage of this experience. Arrian in the second century, commenting on the Celtic practice of hunting with dogs, added that there seemed to be several types including one akin to the Irish wolfhound and another like a bull-mastiff. This might be the breed which Claudius, writing in the fifth century, said could break the necks of great bulls. Earlier, in the third century, Nemesianus indicated that the exporting of dogs was still part of trade and Oppian gave the name of one breed, the Agassian, small, squat and emaciated, but armed with powerful claws and close-set venomous tearing teeth. Its skill was such that it could scent its prey in the air as well as along the ground. These dogs were not used for hunting in packs but kept on the leash before they were released to streak after their prey.

Such a scene is depicted on Castorware pottery where hounds chase hare and deer in vigorous pursuit; in the wilder regions there were opportunities for excellent sport, which delighted army officers. Inscriptions to the hunter god, Vintonius Silvanus, on Scargill Moor (N. Yorks.) testify to the enjoyment of the chase. C. Tetius Veturius Micianus, prefect in charge of the Sebosian cavalry,

dedicated an altar to Silvanus at Bollihope Common, south of Stanhope, Co. Durham, boasting of taking 'a wild boar of remarkable fitness which many of his predecessors had failed to bag'. An angry boar when cornered made dangerous sport; Hadrian broke his collarbone when engaged in a similar hunt. Less dangerous activities were snaring wildfowl or hunting hares, an activity helped by beaters driving them into nets. The figure representing Winter on the Chedworth pavement stumps home, wrapped up well against the cold, hare dangling from his hand ready to be skinned for the pot (**37**).

Fishing was equally important. Catching fish in osier baskets with special-shaped entrances cannot be classified as sport but bronze fishing-hooks found at London, Fishbourne,

37 *The figure of Winter on the seasons' mosaic in the Chedworth villa, Gloucestershire.*

Verulamium and Silchester, together with spears, tridents and other fishing equipment indicate individual prowess. Tridents were useful for catching salmon, which leapt abundantly along certain rivers. The Romans knew this fish in Gaul, and Pliny the Elder had commented on its habits in Aquitania. The Celts held its powers in such respect that it came to personify wisdom, which Finn gained through sucking his fingers burned while cooking the fish. Salmon seems to be the fish depicted on the mosaic found at Lydney on the River Severn, noted still today for its salmon fishing.

38 *On a mosaic found on a villa site at East Coker in Somerset two men carry a deer slung on a pole between them. The hound crouches below to catch the deer's blood.*

Hunting and fishing were country activities (**38**), but the close relationship of country to town meant that many townsmen would indulge their love of sport. Celtic and Roman habits had most satisfactorily merged in these activities. When Pliny the Younger wrote to his friend Caninius Rufus at the turn of the first century AD to ask, 'Are you reading, fishing, hunting or doing all three?', he might equally have asked the same of any friend in Britain, although perhaps his friend would be more likely to do the two latter occupations than the first. Pliny continues, 'I am only vexed at being denied them myself, for I hanker after them as a sick man does for wine, baths and cool springs. . . . New business piles up on the old before the old is finished, and, as more and more links are added to the chain, I still see my work stretching out further and further every day.' This heartfelt cry encapsulates perfectly the work–leisure dilemma across two thousand years.

Public entertainment

The phrase 'bread and circuses' which has come down to us since Roman times summarizes the somewhat cynical attitude of the public authorities towards controlling the lower classes. If food and diversions could be provided for them at a reasonable cost, or even free, there would be fewer reasons for restlessness against the government. Public entertainment could also be a method of siphoning off high spirits although young men were still likely to cause concern. Ammianus Marcellinus grumbles in the fourth century that they were still running riot, galloping horses at 'the speed of the public post' through towns in defiance of a ban on horse racing. It was better to deflect activities and passions into spectator sport and this the Romans, with their genius for organization, were well equipped to do.

The baths

Less robust entertainment came with visits to the baths, where relaxation for tired limbs, diversion through gossip and broadening of knowledge discussing the latest news throughout the empire were combined with cleanliness, social relations and opportunities for material advancement in business deals. The attraction of bathing extended beyond the towns. At posting stations (**colour plate 5**) and settlements around a fort civilians may have been allowed to use the baths, as seems to have been the case at Caerleon where women's hairpins were found in the legionary bath-house.

Civic baths were erected at public expense, usually centrally placed as at Leicester and Caerwent. They were warm, comfortable places, open all day and constantly in use as it would cost more to start up the heating from cold. Both men and women would use them, probably not at the same time, although declarations by Hadrian and Marcus Aurelius in the second century against the custom indicate that mixed bathing did take place. The Leicester baths had an exercise hall on the eastern side, a somewhat rare feature in Britain. Usually baths were adequately furnished with warm and cold baths, changing-rooms and elaborately fitted latrines, a much appreciated amenity.

At Bath (Aquae Sulis) and probably Buxton in Derbyshire, although little is known about the arrangement of that town, both healing and social functions were emphasized. Hot water alleviates pain; when mineral salts are dissolved in it, cures may occur. But there was more to Bath than just the natural elements; there was also the supernatural to consider. The association of the site with the Celtic goddess Sul made inevitable her association with Minerva, goddess of healing. Aquae Sulis attracted soldiers and civilians in search of physical and spiritual well-being and in doing so provided a welcome social amenity. By the end of the first century the huge complex of bathing establishment, theatre and temple was set within a courtyard with superbly decorated screen walls and entered by a magnificent arch.

No expense had been spared. In the nineteenth century the base of the Great Bath was found to be lined with forty-five sheets of lead. Huge quantities of oolite limestone were quarried for the buildings. Statues were placed at the ends of a huge altar. Apollo was needed because of his healing powers; Bacchus was welcomed for he provided people with soporific drink. Jupiter was lord over all, and Hercules was a suitable deity for those who were relaxing after challenging death.

In the Great Bath were found a large number of votive offerings given by suppliants seeking cures. These, however, included curse tablets, so many that it seemed that people came here to alleviate troubled minds or violent tempers by wishing death and destruction to those whom they believed had injured them in a variety of ways. Professional curse writers interpreted dictated threats: 'I have given to Sulis, the goddess, the thief who stole my hooded cloak, be he slave or free, man or woman. Let him not redeem this gift except with his blood.' Someone who hoped that the man who carried off his girlfriend, Vilbia, might 'become as liquid as water' showed a rare wit. The site had more than a local fame. Perigrinus dedicated an altar to Sulis as did Priscus, a stonemason; both had either sought work or were immigrants, the first from Trier, the second from the tribe of the Carnutes, who lived in the Chartres area.

39 *A reconstruction of the theatre at Verulamium. (Drawing by Alan Sorrell)*

Theatres

The association of theatre and religious site was well-known in the Classical world. Plays, recitations and declamations in honour of the gods, and their depiction, comic or serious, was taken as a matter of course. Tacitus' description of the events surrounding the Boudiccan rebellion indicates that Britain had a theatre at Colchester soon after the conquest. At Canterbury, remains indicated a large structure built as early as AD 80 and rebuilt in a more imposing style in the early third century.

The most visible remains today are at Verulamium (**39**). The theatre was constructed as part of the general rebuilding of the town after the disastrous fire of AD 155, when the citizens responded far more quickly than after the Boudiccan rebellion. Building the theatre was an encouraging act by the local council to show its

confidence in the citizens' ability to rebuild and restock.

The theatre has a circular area or orchestra in front of the stage. Three entrances into it were vaulted so that they would bear the wooden seating placed above them buttressed by earth banks. The impression is of a theatre erected in some haste, but twenty years later radical alterations resulted in a more substantial structure. The orchestra was reduced, the stage enlarged and a dressing-room added. Although the stage still had a wooden floor, it was enhanced by a Corinthian-style proscenium as if Classical architecture was now normal practice. Later an ambulatory was built outside the existing exterior wall to allow shelter from the weather, and greater seating accommodation was provided. Seats were often numbered and at Great Chesterford in Essex counters bearing numbers and letters are suggested to be tickets.

Theatres need not be permanent structures. An inscription at Brough-on-Humber refers to a

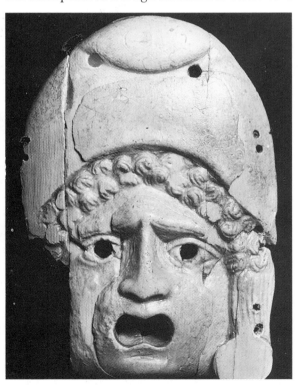

40 *An ivory theatre mask found at Caerleon, Gwent.*

theatre stage. Travelling players might indulge in exhibitions of Celtic bombast or induce an audience to exercise its imagination with the use of a few props. Theatre masks found at Caerleon (**40**) and Baldock hint that Classical-type plays were performed with actors wearing masks to indicate the comic or tragic character they were playing.

Amphitheatres

More robust entertainment took place in the amphitheatre. Those situated near Caerleon and Chester (**41**), and the isolated fort of Tomen-y-Mur (Gwynedd), would be used for military exercises and parades, with perhaps infrequent performances by a travelling entertainment. At Chester a timber amphitheatre, built at the same time as the fort, was later replaced by a stone one. These military amphitheatres had a larger central area than was warranted by the capacity of the seating. Others outside towns had more seating than arena space. Those at Silchester, Carmarthen (Dyfed), Caerwent and Dorchester have been estimated to contain the total population of the towns, which argues for entertainment geared to the lowest common denominator. A small mining community at Charterhouse-on-Mendip in Somerset built one, and two others are attested by inscriptions at Leicester and York. One in London may have served both the military and civilians, as did that at Catterick (N. Yorks.).

The Cirencester amphitheatre indicates how much civil pretensions had increased. Entrance was by passageways, from which access could be gained to the wooden seating set on earthen banks retained by two low stone walls. Wooden shuttering in the passageways was later replaced by stone walls. The town was fortunate in that it could set its amphitheatre in a quarry which supported some of its seating. Elsewhere the banks had been built up. Those at Dorchester, probably constructed in the first century, still stand to a height of about 9m (30ft). Rather unusually there was only one entrance, with opposite to it a room where performers or animals waited before they were sent into the arena. One of the smaller

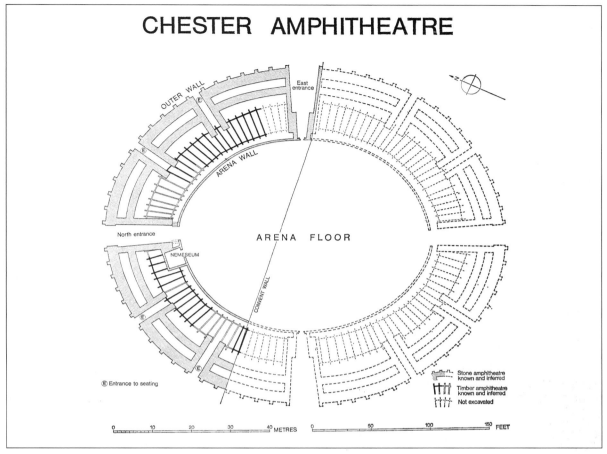

CHESTER AMPHITHEATRE

OUTER WALL

East entrance

ARENA WALL

North entrance

NEMESEUM

ARENA FLOOR

CONVENT WALL

(E) Entrance to seating

Stone amphitheatre known and inferred
Timber amphitheatre known and inferred
Not excavated

0 10 20 30 40 METRES
0 50 100 150 FEET

41 *Plan of the Roman amphitheatre outside the fort at Chester, Cheshire. By the north entrance is a* nemeseum *or shrine to the goddess Nemesis. An altar dedicated to her by the centurion Sextus Marcianus 'as a result of a vision' was found at the back of the room.*

rooms set opposite on the other axis may have held the shrine to Nemesis, goddess of fate, who governed the chance of life and death in the arena.

Gladiators

Roman entertainment had a vicious and cruel element. In the amphitheatres men and animals fought each other in a variety of ways. Fights to the death, particularly appreciated, would have appealed also to the Celts who had had their warlike activities curtailed by the *Pax Romana*. Approval of such fights was not universal. They

were condemned by Varro in the first century BC, while Seneca (died AD 65), who at first approved them, later became repelled by their ferocity. Active opposition and condemnation, however, had to wait until Christianity gained its religious supremacy.

Amphitheatres in Britain may have seen organized gladiatorial fights and a first-century gladiatorial helmet found at Hawkedon in Suffolk was possibly part of the loot seized when Colchester was sacked; veterans at that town would demand displays they had been accustomed to enjoy elsewhere. Gladiators were usually slaves, prisoners of war or criminals. Freeborn men might join them to make their fortunes, for victors of fights could be handsomely rewarded. A law of AD 177 limited the expenses of gladiators to those of labourers' wages (1000–2000 sesterces) but many got far more

61

than this, the most outstanding receiving over 50,000 sesterces. Occasionally women fought in the arena but this was not a regular event. Juvenal is contemptuous of these would-be Amazons, whom he observes dressing up in armour: 'Who has not seen one of them smiting a stump, piercing it through and through with a foil, lunging at it with a shield and going through the proper motions? . . . Unless indeed she is nursing some further ambition in her bosom and is practising for the real arena.'

Gladiators lived apart in their own barracks and had special trainers. One, holding a whip, directs two fights on a mosaic at the Bignor villa in West Sussex, where cupids act out gladiatorial combats: *mirmillones* fight *retiarii*. One has been disarmed, another clutches a wound. On a plaster cast in the museum at Chester, taken from a tombstone (now lost), a *retiarius* advances on an opponent, his attitude recalling Juvenal's sneer in one of his *Satires,* 'See how he wields the trident and when, with trailing right hand he has cast the net in vain, he lifts up his bare face to the benches and flies ... from one end of the arena to the other.'

Gladiatorial scenes were popular on pottery and glassware. A beaker at Colchester depicts Valentinus, a *retiarius,* about to be crushed by the oblong shield of his opponent, Memno, who has the short stabbing sword and helmet of a Samnite (**42**). The names of eight gladiators on a glass cup, also found at Colchester, are a reminder that these men had individual characters as well as having their performances scrutinized for betting purposes. There was a fourth type of gladiator, who does not seem to be represented in Britain. This was the Thracian, who fought with a rounded shield and a curved scimitar.

Managers did not wish to lose their men but public opinion could force a man to kill his opponent. Small wonder that a shrine to Nemesis, often implored to defeat opponents, was included in the amphitheatres of Chester and Caerleon. The writer of a curse tablet found at Caerleon has borrowed or stolen some clothing of his opponent in order to resort to magical practices:

'Lady Nemesis, I give thee a cloak and a pair of boots. Let him who wears them not redeem them except with his life's blood.' Yet these men did not always lead brutal lives. An unnoticed, perhaps doomed, love story comes from Leicester, where scratched on a pottery fragment are the words 'Verecunda actress, Lucius gladiator.'

Other shows

The Colchester beaker also shows Secundus fighting a bear and on another pottery fragment two lions are fighting. Animal fights were much appreciated and the bear mentioned by Martial may have had companions who would not all have been sent to Rome. Bulls and boars could have joined them in British amphitheatres; monster fish, like that depicted on a terracotta plaque at Colchester, probably indicated a farcical contest. Other entertainments could be cockfights, boxing bouts, wrestling matches and acrobatic turns, but there were also spectacles of a more sinister nature. The martyrdom of the Christians Julius and Aaron at Caerleon, may have taken place in the most public of all places of entertainment.

The circus

The third large place of public entertainment was the circus or chariot hippodrome, in which horse, or more likely chariot, racing took place. The Celts, so adept at horsemanship that their prowess was admired by Classical writers, would have watched this form of entertainment with enthusiasm. The circus was more likely to be placed in the open countryside, on a track of cushioning sand, which would have left no trace. The long thin spina, round which the horses raced, and the banked rows of seating, as can still be imagined in the remains of the Circus Maximus in Rome, could have been replaced in Britain by a railed area, two markers and wickerwork stalls for a staggered start. If the markers were placed according to custom the distance covered would be seven laps or 3km (2 miles). Furious jostling took place during the last two laps as the charioteers urged on the horses.

42 *A gladiatorial contest depicted on pottery found at Colchester, Essex. Memno, who wears the helmet of a Samnite, holds his short stabbing sword in his left hand, a characteristic always dreaded by an opponent.*

Chariot racing with a *quadriga* or *biga* was highly organized, providing work for a large number of people. It was spectator entertainment paid for by promoters or as a public duty on festival days by members of the *ordo*. It could be expensive. Juvenal comments: 'Now the spring races are on; the praetor drops his napkin and

63

43 Mosaic of a charioteer driving a quadriga *from the Rudston villa, North Yorkshire.*

44 Relief of a boy-charioteer found at Lincoln. His left arm is extended to grasp the reins and he seems about to raise his right hand in triumph.

sits there in state but those horses just about cost him the shirt off his back one way or another.' As only the first chariot past the post counted and the winner had to build up a sequence of conquests, the will to win was dominant. Opponents were fouled by cutting in, crowding out and whipping their horses. A bad accident, called a shipwreck, could result in the death of a driver or a horse.

Even if no masonry remains have been found in Britain, there are hints that chariot racing took place. On a mosaic pavement found at Horkstow in Humberside is a spirited contest; one *biga* is about to have an accident as it turns the corner of the spina. A wheel flies from a chariot and an attendant runs fruitlessly to catch the falling driver. Another chariot tips up as the driver fights to control it. A mosaic pavement at the Rudston villa shows the driver of a *quadriga* galloping headlong towards the spectator. His pleasure is obvious for he carries the palm and wreath of victory (**43**).

At first there were two colours, red and white, then blue and green were added. It is the red which is victorious at Horkstow. Domitian added two further colours, purple and gold, but eventually blue and green absorbed the others. At the Chedworth villa someone seems to have scratched on a wall his reminder of a bet on the greens. The sensitive carving at Lincoln (**44**) of a young boy, eyes fixed on his left hand holding the reins, is a reminder that the sport attracted the young and adventurous, as Juvenal implies: 'The races are fine for young men; they can cheer their fancy and bet at long odds and sit with some smart little girlfriend but I'd rather let my wrinkled skin soak up this mild spring sunshine.'

1 *Hadrian's Wall strides over the landscape keeping to the crest of the Whin Sill: view from Cuddy's Crag looking east.*

2 *An imaginative view of the interior of one of the huts in the Maiden Castle hill-fort, Dorset. The family is grouped around the fire over which a cauldron hangs; in the background is an oven. The Romans destroyed all the huts and moved the inhabitants to the new town of Dorchester.* (Drawn by Paul Birkbeck; copyright: English Heritage)

3 *An appreciation of the higher branches of learning could be depicted in mosaics. The owner of the Low Ham villa, Dorset, had approved a design showing the story of Dido and Aeneas.*

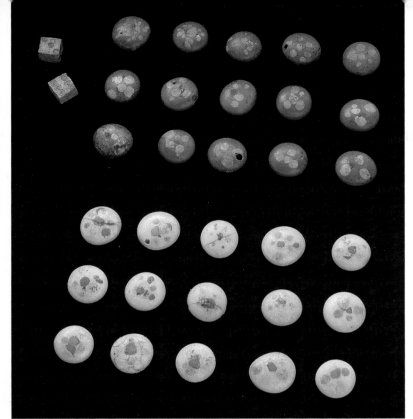

4 *Fifteen red and fifteen white gaming counters and two dice found in the mausoleum at Lullingstone, Kent; gaming board, counters and dice found at Corbridge, Northumberland.*

5 *A small station and a set of baths were established for the imperial post in the first century at Wall, Staffordshire, alongside Watling Street. (Drawn by Claire Thorne; copyright: English Heritage)*

6 *Reconstruction of the Lullingstone villa in Kent as it might have appeared in AD 350. The main building has a small bath-house attached on the left. A room in the wing on the right side was converted into a Christian chapel by the owner. Behind the villa is a small mausoleum built on the terraced hillside. (Drawn by Graham Sumner; copyright: English Heritage)*

7 *Reconstruction of a butcher's shop.*
(Drawn by Judith Dobie; copyright:
English Heritage)

8 *Two loaves baked in the shape of those*
produced by a Roman baker.

9 *Cornelian intaglio with a depiction of Victory writing on a shield, found in the Lullingstone Roman villa, Kent.*

10 *Reconstruction of the latrine in the fort of Housesteads on Hadrian's Wall.* (Copyright: Peter Connolly)

11 *Huge amounts of firewood were needed to stoke the Wroxeter baths in Shropshire. Calculations for the small baths at Welwyn suggest that 114 tonnes of firewood, a denuding of 23 hectares (57 acres) would be required each year.* (Drawn by Ivan Lapper; copyright: English Heritage)

12 *Mosaic with geometrical decoration found in a second-century house at Aldborough, North Yorkshire.*

13 *Decorating the Lullingstone villa. A mosaic-worker lays out part of the pavement, while his companion cuts up a tile to make tesserae. In the background one man prepares plaster ready for his fellow-worker to skim the wall preparatory to fresco painting.* (Drawn by Graham Sumner; copyright: English Heritage)

4
Domestic housing

Owner occupation and renting

In the Mediterranean part of the Roman world the majority of houses seem to have been rented but little evidence is available for Britain. It is possible that in country areas 'owner occupation' might consist of the wooden house or aisled hall added to by subsequent generations. More usual was renting a house or a room in a town or even in a villa.

Investment in land and housing provided profits and in Britain the native aristocracy would be encouraged to invest as much as possible in order to have a stake in the established order. But houses could be flimsily built with few repairs being done. Cicero wrote to Atticus in the first century BC: 'Two of my shops have fallen down and the rest are cracking; so not only have the tenants fled but even the mice have migrated.' What appears to be a shamefaced letter is contradicted in the next line, 'Other people call it a calamity, but I don't count it even a nuisance', especially, one suspects, if it gave him an opportunity to get rid of the tenants and rebuild. However, elsewhere Cicero discusses the question of property being offered for sale, which has certain features – vermin-ridden, insanitary, liability to collapse – which the owner knows about but no one else. If the owner sells this property without telling the purchaser he is acting dishonestly.

Fire was always a problem. In first-century AD Rome, Nero decreed that everyone should have something in their house which would help to dowse a fire. In Britain, besides minor fires, conflagrations burned down the fora of Verulamium and Wroxeter necessitating widespread rebuilding. Each ward in a town was supposed to have its own fire brigade, which patrolled at night with axes and fire buckets, but primitive equipment could do very little. Vitruvius, in the early first century AD, said that once a fire caught hold the houses would 'catch fire like torches'. Only wholesale destruction of adjoining shops and houses could stop the fires from spreading. If someone pulled down a neighbour's house to create a fire barrier, he could not be liable for a damage suit if his action was out of concern for the general good. The flimsy structure of the buildings meant that rebuilding was comparatively easy, but the anguish of the occupants watching their precious possessions being burned would be considerable.

Property

Property was usually sublet so that many parts of a town would become very crowded. In Britain a large amount of land might be available in town centres but building would be dictated by the area within the defences. Under Roman law, land use was carefully controlled. If Britain did adhere to the law, then commercial property had to be used for commerce and residential property for residence. This would certainly have applied in the early years of the empire although by the fourth century restrictions may have been relaxed as more people flooded into the towns.

Under Roman law a person owned property from the land to the sky. Thus a property could not be divided and sold in horizontal portions, although if there was an upper storey the owner could let it. The sixth-century *Codex Iustinianus*, a compilation of earlier Roman law, decreed that if a person could prove that he owned the lower storey of a building then there was no doubt that the upper storey belonged to him also, even if it had been built by a neighbour, who was trying to extend his property laterally. If buildings were in multiple occupancy, as seemingly was the case with some of the villas, the owners would have divided the property vertically. In aisled houses in the country or on the outskirts of towns, a different set of laws based on native custom would prevail.

Owners of property who wished to develop sites could evict tenants and subtenants but, on the whole, tenants would be treated with respect. Under Roman law no money had to be paid in advance until the end of the lease or at the end of the property year, the last day of June. Owners had the right to inspect the premises before that date so that the month of June was a nerve-racking one for both tenant and landlord, resulting in a higher rent, an eviction or a compromise arrangement.

Houses and shops

Many people in towns lived above or at the rear of shops; others lived away from their premises. Given the relatively small size of British towns and their proximity to an outside community, some people would live outside the town making a daily journey to work, or, in the reverse direction, to oversee their farmland.

Commercial properties might take the form of strip houses, such as those excavated at Verulamium and London. Goods would be displayed in an open-front shop, secured by shutters at night. In London, doorways in the side walls opened into narrow alleys between the buildings, suggesting that these buildings were not occupied by a single family but were let to several tenants, probably of a new artisan class who had moved into London seeking work. Brickearth or lime was painted on the external surfaces to protect against the weather. Tiled-built hearths set against an internal wall or in the centre of the room provided cooking and heating facilities. Many premises, rebuilt after the Boudiccan fire, were replaced in the second or third century.

Wings could be added to form a courtyard. Early houses at Gloucester had foundation sleeper walls of stone and clay, supporting timber and wattle and daub walls, consisting of puddled clay and dung bound together with straw and horsehair. Internal partitions of wood were set on wooden sills although occasionally there was a shallow stone foundation. During the second century these flimsy structures were gradually replaced by walls of mortared masonry and floors of mortar and packed clay, on which straw, rushes or textiles might be placed. In other houses tiles or timber floors were laid. Change of use and occupier might be shown by the establishment of small industries such as ironworking furnaces.

Later still, one small house in Gloucester was replaced by a house with three or four wings, set around a paved courtyard, enhanced by a fountain and a water system. Passageways led to the street, and the wings, each containing several rooms linked by a veranda, were soundly constructed. Floors were of mortar and one boasted a mosaic floor, a fashion copied by other houses. Once one neighbour laid a mosaic, others might follow suit spurred on by admiration or envy. The ephemeral nature of the housing, however, is shown by the fact that in the third century the house was pulled down and the site was left vacant.

Excavation of houses in Silchester revealed that simple rectangular buildings of four or five rooms were extended to become winged houses with rooms entered from a veranda. A courtyard created by adding a wall makes a house face in on itself, offering both privacy for social activities and protection against the weather.

Heating arrangements could be very efficient. Under-heating was done by hypocausts (**45**).

45 *A hypocaust in the Chedworth villa.*

Channels in the form of a 'union jack pattern' were set into the concrete floor or the floor might be placed on pillars of brick and tile. A furnace, stoked from outside, heated the air in these and in box-tiles plastered internally in rows vertically up the walls. The whole arrangement provided an efficient central-heating system, which would arouse a desire to emulate. In many houses only one room appears to have been heated in this manner which suggests that the system was expensive. It also assumes that there would be one room where the occupants gathered on cold days, ensuring a form of community living. One or two houses had a bath-suite added, an even greater attraction, much as a private swimming pool today adds a further dimension to an enhanced life-style.

Houses did have windows. Some window openings have been found in cellars, and a ground-floor window at Dorchester had splayed sides. Windows were glazed with pieces of bluish-green glass, held in place by iron or wooden grills. Stout wooden outer doors had a padlock or a more complicated tumbler lock. A simple latch would secure interior doors, but often a curtain would suffice to cut out draughts.

Thatching and reeds provided simple roofs; other roofs were constructed from flanged tiles over which semicircular ones were placed. Both of these tapered slightly so that a tile would naturally overlap the one below. Their weight held them in place but they could be mortared on a steeply pitched roof. Gable ends might have decorated tiles on them. In some areas, as in Northamptonshire, stone was the natural roofing material.

Courtyard houses would have a garden in the centre, laid out in a formal manner with box-hedging and dog-roses. At Silchester one or two piles of debris contained box-clippings mixed with elder and weeds revealing where a gardener had been at work. Even in a town fruit trees could be grown – apple, damson, plum and the more exotic medlar. A vegetable garden would also be considered a necessity.

Roundhouses

The usual form of house in pre-Roman Britain appears to have been the roundhouse, an ubiquitous style which continued in rural areas. Walls would be of timber or of timber posts with wattle panels. These could be replaced with stone foundations supporting the timber frame as happened at Overstone (Northants). Roofs were of thatch or turves. If these reached to the ground like the one at Whitton in South Glamorgan they provided a run-off for rain but also a run-up for mice and other vermin. Aerial photographs of the Nene valley have revealed hundreds of homesteads and small huts set within circular or rectilinear enclosures. Similar evidence comes from the Cheviots, on the border between Scotland and England.

Such a life-style might be considered one to be endured rather than welcomed. That it was acceptable is indicated by the fact that there was constant rebuilding. At Odell (Beds.) two circular houses, each of which was twice rebuilt, were constructed at the beginning of the first century AD within a D-shaped enclosure. These were abandoned at the end of the century only to be built in similar form, 100m (328ft) to the south. Several generations of one family group lived in these houses until the fourth century. Even then they were not abandoned when a small villa was built to one side, as if one generation had finally accepted a more Romanized life-style or if they had become part of a larger estate with a bailiff installed on the premises.

Villas

A great variety of housing can be considered under the name 'villa', which usually implies some form of farming establishment. A small house might add outbuildings, so that the term might describe anything from a cottage to a grand estate. Some villas show signs of continuity. The owner of an Iron Age hut might refuse to leave the house which his father had built, but his sons could become increasingly frustrated with his attitude. Within two generations more comfortable accommodation was constructed. This might have been the case at Park Street (Herts.) where a Belgic farmstead was rebuilt in timber, then remodelled in the later first century as a stone-built house with five rooms, a veranda and a cellar. The veranda, an advanced architectural feature, allows easy communication to rooms as well as ensuring privacy.

In Kent, villas may have been established by merchants from Gaul preferring to live near their business interests in London or at the port of entry. One at Eccles, founded about AD 65, was based on a type of hall-villa, already established in Gaul, comprising a large central hall used for both living- and working-quarters, set between two rooms of equal size. Owners of establishments in the Darenth valley exploited their interests; coal from the Durham area stoked a bath-house furnace at Northfleet.

Sometimes owners embarked on enterprises to which they were not fully committed. A farmstead, excavated at Whitton, was occupied for about 300 years but it was not until the mid-second century that the first masonry building appeared. Painted wallplaster shows some pretensions to a Romanized life-style but the two hypocausts added to heat the rooms were never fired, as if the owners had lost the will to achieve a higher standard of living.

It was in the southern regions of Britain that the greatest enthusiasm for building to greater comfort standards was most obvious. Single ranges of buildings were added to produce courtyard homes and in the fourth century came a rash of rebuilding resulting in complexes of three or four wings grouped around a central area, a yard or a garden (**colour plate 6**). They were not in any sense farmyards. Animals and workers were housed elsewhere, often in aisled barn-like structures. The largest villas, such as that at North Leigh, had about forty rooms (**46**);

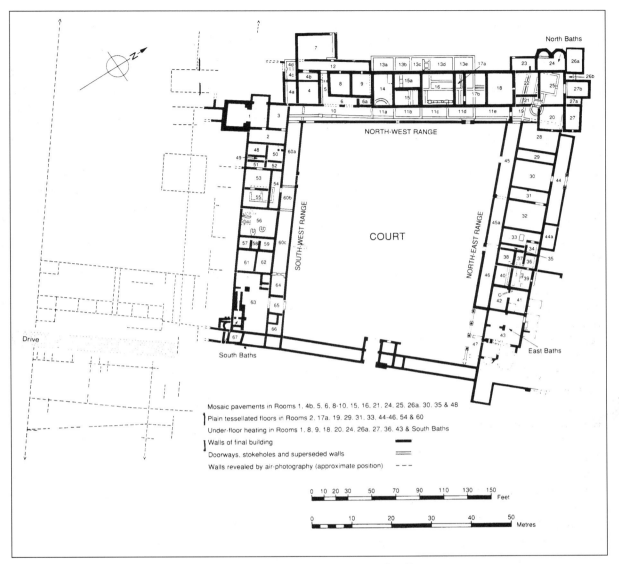

North Baths

7

4d
4c
4b
12   13a 13b 13c 13d 13e 17a   23   24   26a
4a   4   5   9   14   15a   26b
6   16   18   22   25   27b
6a   11a 11b 11c 11d 11e   21   20   27a
1   3   10   19
2   27

NORTH-WEST RANGE

49
48 50 60a
51 52
53   45
54   COURT   29
55 60b   30   44
                31
56   32   45a
57 58 59 60c   33   44a
61 62   34
64   38 37 36 35
63 65   46 40 39
66   42 41
67   c
South Baths   47   43   East Baths

Drive

SOUTH-WEST RANGE

NORTH-EAST RANGE

Mosaic pavements in Rooms 1, 4b, 5, 6, 8-10, 15, 16, 21, 24, 25, 26a, 30, 35 & 48
Plain tessellated floors in Rooms 2, 17a, 19, 29, 31, 33, 44-46, 54 & 60
Under-floor heating in Rooms 1, 8, 9, 18, 20, 24, 26a, 27, 36, 43 & South Baths
Walls of final building
Doorways, stokeholes and superseded walls
Walls revealed by air-photography (approximate position)

0 10 20 30   50   70   90   110   130 150
                                      Feet

0   10   20   30   40   50
                                      Metres

46 *Plan of the North Leigh villa in Oxfordshire in its final development in the fourth century.*

Chedworth and Box (Wilts.) about thirty. The south-western part of Britain seems to have attracted architects and craftsmen who built and decorated in the Classical style. At least sixty villas include apsed dining-rooms, some, like that at Keynsham, Avon, of a sophisticated hexagonal pattern. The capitals of the colonnaded veranda were finished in Corinthian style, while moulded pilasters, decorated cornices and balustrades provided architectural sophistication.

Division of villas

Until recently the assumption has been that a villa belonged to one family. Plans of some villas, however, suggest that they may be two or more parts of an economic whole, with the division indicated by the placing of a water tank, or a shrine utilizing the concept of protection at the place of contact. The theory may have substance if the term 'extended family' is used rather than 'nuclear family'. The Gayton Thorpe villa, Norfolk, may be two houses or occupation units, each having a portico or wing room, placed side by side, but joined by a connecting block to form

47 *The reconstruction in the Corinium Museum of a Roman living-room in a town house in Cirencester.*

a whole. Two families might live here, even perhaps a marriage where the man had two wives, each with a separate family.

The villa at Great Witcombe in Gloucestershire has a north range acting as a corridor, with only a single room in the middle and two larger houses situated to one side. At North Wraxall (Wilts.), on the other hand, a large central hall dominating a series of small rooms could mean that the extended family continued the tradition of a Celtic social group living together.

Interior decoration

Personality of people is revealed by interior decoration and fittings (**47**). A casual glance around a room is enough to give some clue to likes and dislikes, style and taste and, usually, to social class. In Britain people liked their houses to have painted plaster walls, the brighter the better, perhaps even gaudy. At Silchester panels of plain colour, in particular red and yellow, were favoured, although the panels might be dotted or veined in another colour, as for example grey veined with blue. Borders of a deeper colour were common. A love of nature is apparent. One dado consisted of a dark red band with a black band below and a green one above. On the red band, ears of yellow barley point towards lilac quatrefoils, and circles of green have leaves jutting from them. Fashionable walls included imitation marbling, painted pillars, garlands, candelabra and vegetables.

Excavation of a house at Verulamium produced an almost complete wall. On a purple ground were cream-coloured columns, with in between an imitation wall veneer in green, purple, yellow and red. A dado below consisted of small rectangles outlined in green below the columns. In another house a ceiling was of purple with a latticework of wheat ears enclosing flowers and birds. The walls of the corridors seem to have been of red decorated with candelabra. The total effect is one of sombre competence.

Floors were made of brick, tiles, mortar, *opus signinum* (white cement with crushed brick polished to a shine) and tesserae. The shell mosaic at Verulamium was obviously chosen for its pattern, but the horned deity might have deeper significance. The numerous Orpheus pavements in the Cirencester region suggest selection by a cult. The coldness of the marble might be alleviated by woven textiles but the 'seasons' pavement at Cirencester served as a series of decorated 'rugs', which the inhabitants would not wish to conceal.

Furniture

Furniture might be scarce. Martial says that in Rome a poor man had a toga, a hearth, a bug-ridden bed, rush mat, lock and key, and a cup. Substitute tunic for toga and this could be a house in Britain. One Briton might be like Codrus, mentioned by Juvenal as having a bed, cupboard, pitcher and a chest. When Martial's Vacerra moves house he takes his bed, table, lantern and wooden bowl with him. Locks and keys, however, do suggest that protection was needed to prevent stealing even a small number of possessions.

A more intricate interior, carved on the sarcophagus found at Simpelveldt in Holland, reveals what a well-furnished house might have (**48**). The lady herself is depicted on a sturdy couch comfortably ensconced on a mattress, stuffed with reeds or wool. A light mattress alone might serve as a bed. More elaborate couches are seen on funerary reliefs at York and Chester. Aelia Aeliana reclines with her husband on a firmly stuffed mattress placed on a couch which has curved ends and legs. Couches could have backs and sides and be comfortably fitted with leather cushions. Rugs, skins and lengths of woven cloth would serve as blankets.

The basket chair had a long history being used in the Iron Age. A Romano-British example can be seen on the Murrell Hill tombstone (**49**). On a relief at Cirencester the mother goddess rests her feet on a square footstool. Children, like the slave of Candida Barita at York, stood on footstools to see what was going on. Men might sit on folding stools; those found in the tombs at Bartlow and Holborough are of iron with bronze decoration. A reconstruction of the latter suggests that it had a leather seat; wooden stools were common or even pieces of tree trunk in poorer homes. In rural communities people were more used to squatting on their haunches or sitting on rugs or skins. Other furniture would be tripod tables similar to that on the tombstone of Aelia Aeliana. At Silchester and Dorchester people could buy shale tables, made with elaborate decoration of lions' heads, and other household equipment such as trays.

Fittings survive to show that cupboards, chests and caskets were common in Britain. These could be locked but the most secure place is the hidden one. One of the houses at Silchester had a cavity dug into the floor into which a strong-box had been sunk; inside were the remains of strap hinges which had held the lid, the lock-plate and the key, covered with a mat over a wooden fitting. This must have kept the valuables as secure as anything could do in that town.

Rooms would need to be lit. Lamps, introduced after the conquest, were stamped with traditional Classical designs; gladiatorial contests and deities were popular. A bronze one found in the Thornborough barrow (Bucks.) had a removable lid with a chain attached to prevent it getting lost. A particularly splendid one found in the Thames at Greenwich had two nozzles and a curved reared handle ending in a ram's head. A twisted piece of cloth, impregnated with oil to act as a wick, would burn for about two hours, although this would be expensive if imported olive-oil was used. Candlesticks were also in use. An iron one from Great Chesterford has three crudely made animal limbs but another from London had three splendid paws. Wax or tallow

candles were placed in a holder stuck by its spike to the wall. One problem in using candles or wicks is that, unless they are made of pure wax or used with pure olive-oil, they give off a strong smell and pieces of soot. Another is that flickering light soon tires the eyes. People in both town and country would get up with the sun in order to make full use of daylight hours.

Homes without a hypocaust needed some heating. Less sophisticated homes would have a hearth on the floor and let the smoke go where it would. In some of the villas wall recesses may indicate the presence of a chimney; some at Sparsholt, Hampshire, and Newport on the Isle of Wight had a corbelled hood. But the main

48 *A lady buried in an elaborate sarcophagus at Simpelveldt in Holland, had her living-room furniture carved on its inner sides. The carving at the foot of the bed has been suggested to represent a bath-house, having small upper windows and a heated room on the left.*

form of heating was the portable brazier. Burnt patches on the floors of houses in Silchester testify to this use. It could also be dangerous, not so much because of setting fire to the house but because in rooms sealed against the cold there was always the possibility of carbon monoxide poisoning, a fate which almost killed the Emperor Julian (AD 361–3) and certainly did kill the Emperor Jovian (AD 363–4).

72

49 *An tombstone of a lady from Murrell Hill, Carlisle. She wears a long tunic over which a shawl has been thrown. Her small child tenderly caresses a pet bird.*

5
Food, drink and eating habits

Celtic diet

Occasionally there has been a tendency to transpose Roman or Italianate cookery habits and the recipes of one known Roman cookery book to Romano-British society. The Roman Cookery Book of Apicius (*De Re Coquinaria*), a compilation of recipes and gastronomic hints, possibly by several authors, is often quoted in accounts of Roman Britain as if the population dined on gourmet meals. A more accurate picture may be gained from archaeological evidence and from contemporary literary evidence taken from sources other than Apicius.

For the inhabitants of both Iron Age Britain and rural Roman Britain, food availability would depend on the seasons and on the area. The usual methods of preserving food by salting, soaking in brine, drying, smoking and smearing with honey were well known. Ears of wheat and barley, stored during the winter in deep pits covered with a clay dome, were ground when required either by the saddle quern, or by the rotary quern introduced in the late first century BC. Modern grinding experiments produced 0.45kg (1lb) of flour an hour; in India a skilled operator produces an output of 1.8kg (4lb) an hour. The grain is put twice through the quern since one passage leaves the grain half-ground.

In winter, life would be hard especially in the northern regions and, if the weather was bad, famine conditions prevailed. Certainly people would be less likely to reject food of any kind. But in summer, much would be obtained from the wild. Fruits and berries indigenous to Britain include wild raspberries, blackberries, elderberries, wood strawberries, crab-apples and bullaces, all a welcome addition to the diet.

The diet would be rich in fat and protein in the summer, less so in winter when food was scarce. Carbohydrate content would also be high, although pieces of pork, beef, mutton, even horseflesh, and fish added to a pottage of ground beans and wheat or oats provide protein. Domesticated chickens would provide eggs. A lack of vitamin C would make scurvy a constant threat. Calcium content would be higher in summer because of the greater availability of fresh milk. A mainly cereal diet, however, contains phytate and fibre; the consumption of these components interferes with the absorption of calcium thus predisposing individuals to rickets and osteomalacia. Both diseases have been found in skeletons excavated in Romano-British cemeteries and it is unlikely that the Celtic population was not similarly afflicted. Vitamin D is also essential for the uptake and utilization of calcium in the skeleton structure. Egg yolks, liver and fish oils would provide this but the best source is the action of sunlight on the skin, and lack of sun could be a problem in northern regions.

The inhabitants of Iron Age and rural Roman Britain would certainly be aware of the abundance of plants, roots and other crops useful to them. Even if they did not understand the science of nutrition they would know what they liked, what made them feel well, what was harmful to

50 *A mosaic in the Square of the Corporations at Ostia, the port of Rome, depicting a man carrying an amphora over his shoulder crossing the gangplank of a boat.*

them, giving them a palatable diet of foods associated with texture, smell, colour and taste: savoury, sweet, neutral. This food choice would provide, perhaps incidently, protein, vitamins, minerals and calories. When more meat and fruit became available, consumption of these products would increase with a consequent decrease in the consumption of cereals and roots. Times of plenty meant gorging of food, but at other times it would be difficult to know from where the next meal would come. Gorging for its own sake or even gourmet eating can only take place in times of affluence. These would come once the Roman administration had established itself in Britain.

Even before the conquest native British products had been supplemented by trade with Rome, altering eating and cooking habits. Some indication of products brought in by trade comes from a study of the different forms and quantity of amphorae, a most convenient form of container, seemingly ungainly, but useful for stacking and easily portable in wicker or straw containers. Amphorae were sealed by a bung secured by mortar; one of oak from Silchester had a gash on it made by the tool prising it out. Two men could carry one slung from a pole with ropes through the handle, or one man could carry it on his shoulder (**50**). It could hold up to 4.5 litres (1 gallon) and alteration in shape according to area and period provides dating evidence.

Roman tastes – wine

Although wine was imported in wooden casks and barrels – silver-fir barrels from Aquitaine were found in Silchester and reused barrels from the Rhineland lined wells in London – most of it was carried in amphorae. Athenaeus says, 'The drink of [Celtic] wealthier classes is of wine imported from Italy . . . This is unadulterated but sometimes a little water is added.' Wine was flavoured with herbs, but could have a distinctive taste because the interior of amphorae was sometimes coated with bitumen, wood pitch or resin. Pottery fragments found at Silchester indicate that the townspeople received wine of this type.

Amphorae fragments found at the Sheepen site, Colchester, indicate that large quantities of wine were entering Britain by AD 5 and that after the conquest the site was supplied by wine from at least nineteen different sources, at first from Italy but then from the Iberian provinces, Rhodes, Sicily, the Rhineland and southern Gaul (**51**). North Africa became the main supply area once the Spanish trade had been disrupted by the Germanic invasion of AD 260. Amphorae sherds in London prove that by AD 50 wine was being brought up the Thames, and at Canterbury small quantities of wine were imported from the eastern Mediterranean and the Dodecanese.

51 *Different types of amphorae as arranged in the Rheinisches Landesmuseum, Mainz.*

52 *Conversation at a wine shop.*

Some of the amphorae contained defructum, a viscous, sweet produce when the must or grape juice is boiled to evaporate the water. It was used like honey or added to improve poor wine. As it was manufactured in lead pans it might have resulted in serious lead poisoning. At Verulamium one shop had a large number of broken amphorae in it suggesting wine had been sold there. Close by was a cellar where scratches on the walls were made by the pointed ends of amphorae being dragged along the floor (**52**).

Amphorae contents

Other products carried in amphorae include plums, according to markings on an amphora at the fort of Brough-on-Noe, figs and dates, both useful sources of fibre and iron. Fig seeds have been found at London, Silchester and Verulamium, probably imported as dried fruit because figs need a pollinating insect, the caprificatory wasp, which was not present in Roman Britain. Carbonized dates were found at Colchester in the remains of a building burned in the Boudiccan rebellion in AD 60.

Early imports of olive-oil are found at Sheepen, Canterbury, Silchester and Verulamium. Amphorae could hold large quantities: one recovered intact from the Thames Estuary contained 6000 olive stones, the remains of excellent Posean olives. Olive-oil was imported on a regular basis from Spain, especially from Tarraconensis and Baetica, reputed to be the best oil available, then from North Africa. Its use must indicate a change in dietary habits. Athenaeus had said that 'the Celts do not use olive-oil because of its scarcity and because it appears unpleasant to them'. The army imported it in great quantities and its versatility as a cooking agent was obvious and acceptable. It was also used for lighting, lubrication and sealing wood.

A product alien to Britain was the fish-sauce, liquamen or garum, an acquired taste which soon become popular. Liquamen was made from the entrails of anchovies, and garum from tunny fish,

but the terms are interchangeable. It was an essential part of Roman culinary taste, enhancing a flavour (somewhat as Worcestershire or soy sauces do) or blending tastes, which is a feature of the present Far Eastern fish-sauces. One amphora found at Southwark, London, indicated that the finest fish-sauce from Antipolis (Antibes) was imported into Britain.

At Canterbury the sauce importation ceased in the early second century but so essential was it that local industries began. Excavations on the Roman waterfront in London uncovered a third-century reused fish-sauce amphora of a type associated with the importation of herring and sprat, indigenous to northern European waters. Deposits of fish bones at York and Lincoln also indicate that those towns produced fish-sauce on a commercial basis. This salt diet can lead to high blood pressure but its effects would have been mitigated by hard work.

Fish

Juvenal's comments that British oysters were a favoured delicacy in Rome show that their transportation was no problem to traders, and large quantities of oyster shells from Romano-British sites suggest it was one of the fast foods of the Roman world. Mussels, cockles, whelks and snails were equally acceptable; the *cocleare,* with a pointed end, was devised to prize them from their shells. At Caerwent one shop has been identified as selling shellfish, and bathers in the fortress baths at Caerleon patronized a shellfish bar.

Bones found on other sites show that both fresh- and salt-water fish were eaten. The citizens of York ate pike and eel from the Ouse, herring and sea-bream from coastal waters, and salmon and smelt, when in season. Whale bones at Bishopstone, West Sussex, suggest that stranded whales provided an unexpected form of food supply.

Introduction of horticultural practice

Foods imported into Britain and soon becoming part of the practice of horticulture included herbs (aniseed, mint, parsley, rosemary, dill, thyme), vegetables (fennel, cabbage, onions, broad-beans, lettuce, peas, leeks, cucumber, turnip, carrots) and nuts (walnuts, almonds, sweet chestnut). Small and stringy vegetables, pounded in mortars to soften them, also provided fibre. Fruits included the domesticated plum, sweet cherry and damson, soon becoming established as cultivated crops. Pliny the Elder said that cherry trees had been taken to Britain as early as AD 47. Peach and cherry stones have been found in London and medlar stones, elderberry and mulberry seeds at Silchester.

There was some attempt to grow grapes. Evidence of vine cultivation was found at the Boxmoor villa (Herts.), and a failed vineyard has been suggested at North Thoresby (Lincs.), although reconsideration of the evidence may point to an orchard. Grape pips at Silchester and Doncaster in South Yorkshire are either imported raisins or the residue of winemaking. At Brockley Hill, to the north of London, local potters produced a type of amphora, coated internally with a resin, which could have bottled a locally produced wine, possibly from the Verulamium region. One thousand four hundred seeds, which would give a quantity of 150–300 apples, found in a pit at Doncaster, may be the remains of a fermented apple drink.

Meat

Better breeding of cattle would increase the quality and quantity of meat, milk, butter and cheese. Examination of bones found on military and civilian sites indicate methods of butchery. Modern butchery practice is to split a hung carcass down the axis, then quarter it, removing the limbs in sections. The Romans placed the whole carcass flat, then removed each limb in preparation to being further divided. Heavy knives and cleavers would make short work of this. There does not seem to have been any boning of the joint. Marks on bones suggest meat was scraped off, perhaps even shredded. At Neatham, in Hampshire, badly chopped shoulder blades indicate heavy, unskilled butchery. Bones were split to extract the marrow and to be boiled for broth.

At York, where over 20,000 bones have been studied, there seems to be systematic butchery on a commercial scale during the late second and early third centuries with beef, including smoked and cured joints, predominating; young lambs and piglets were also slaughtered.

At Cirencester several pits in one building were filled with sawn bones, possibly remains from a meat market. A row of shops opposite was equipped with large ovens; two had wells and the excavators suggested that the shops prepared and sold cooked meats. One shop at Verulamium was identified as a butcher's shop where flesh, perhaps for sausages, had been stripped from dismembered horses before the bones were buried on the site; lamb-skull fragments in a ditch at Southwark and cattle bones in a pit in London also indicate butchers' shops (**colour plate 7**).

Quantification of animal bone in the first century AD reveals a more dominant beef and pork diet in towns in preference to sheep and goat on military sites. However, in the more remote areas preference had to give way to availability. Hare and deer were hunted and there was the occasional consumption of dog. Bones of pigeon, partridge and pheasant have been found. Ducks and chickens were fattened for table, and the Roman author Columella (first century AD) says geese can be reared with little trouble, providing they have plenty of water. Bones of peacock and swan suggest more exotic tastes. Their meat, oily and strongly tasting, is best minced for rissoles. At York and Silchester bones of the edible frog have been found. York also produced bones of the garden dormice, perhaps imported as a delicacy, in which case Apicius' recipe for stuffed dormouse would prove useful!

Grain and bread

Some areas still depended on a high-cereal diet. Ears of wheat, roasted before threshing, prevented sprouting and killed off pests, as well as making the hulls brittle so that grain could be released by pounding. Grain was still milled by the rotary quern, which was often imported from the Andernach lava region of the Rhineland. Stone-milled flour, relatively high in vitamin B, produces a course-grain sticky-crumb bread when baked (**colour plate 8**). Sieving takes out the bran, but evidence from the Bearsden fort, near Glasgow, shows that whole-grain bread with poppy seeds was acceptable to the troops and would have provided a high-fibre diet. Literary evidence confirms archaeology for Pliny the Elder records that wholemeal flour was flavoured with coriander and opium poppy seeds, while Petronius (first century AD) sneered at one guest who asked for wholemeal bread because it was nourishing and prevented constipation.

This type of bread soon goes hard and has to be baked daily. Both grinding and baking would be a constant task for the household, if it could not buy loaves from a town baker. The latter made use of a donkey mill and remains of these at London and Hamworthy in Dorset indicate a commercial form of milling was practised. This mill had a conical base over which an hour-glass-shaped hopper, held by a spindle, was turned by horses or slaves. Flour milling on a commercial scale was noted at Silchester, where a hopper spindle and bases for rotary mills have been found in one building.

Town bakers used brick ovens, heated internally with wood or charcoal. The ashes were raked out, the bread, in the shape of flat rounded loaves, put in and the mouth sealed. Bakery shops are hard to identify but two sites suggested are at Springhead in Kent and Holditch in Staffordshire. A pastry cook's mould has been found at Silchester and an iron slice for removing bread from the oven was found at Verulamium. Bread can also be baked in flat earthenware pots; another pot placed over the dough causes it to rise by the steam-baking process (**53**).

Barley was used for animal fodder. Quantities purchased for Vindolanda suggest that it was used as fodder, for brewing or to replace corn at the end of the season. Soldiers did not like barley bread, probably because it was a heavy bread with a greyish tinge, soon becoming unpalatable and mouldy. In the early second century AD

53 *An unleavened loaf (compare with* **colour plate 8***).*

Suetonius reports that the Emperor Augustus disgraced any legion which failed to fight well by having every tenth man executed and putting the survivors on an exclusive diet of barley bread.

Dioscorides, in the first century AD, mentioned that a drink called *curmi*, a light barley ale, was often drunk instead of wine, but he noted with disapproval that it caused headaches. In Britain and Spain a wheaten beer was preferred; grains of barley have been found at Caerleon and Verulamium. At York a huge granary containing barley became so infested with grain beetle, probably brought in with imported grain, that the ground layer had to be sealed and the building dismantled. Oats provided the Roman cavalry with fodder, and rye in the northern areas provided a heavier grain.

Eating habits

It was customary for the Romans, copying Greek habits, to take their meals reclining on couches, a custom indicated by funerary banqueting scenes and the terracotta figures from a child's grave at Colchester humorously representing reclining diners and entertainers at a banquet (**54**). Other diners take their meals seated upright around a table, as portrayed on reliefs in Gaul and the Rhineland.

Roman eating habits, apart from the gargantuan banquets, were sensible and abstemious. Breakfast was as it implied, breaking the night fast with a little fruit and bread, often dipped in wine. Lunch was a snack of vegetables, meat and

54 *Terracotta figurines found in a child's grave at Colchester are caricatures of diners and reciters at a banquet. Each reciter holds a tray on which is a partly unrolled scroll.*

bread. It would be in the evening, when relaxing after work had finished, that the main meal (*cena*) would be eaten. This comprised three courses. An hors-d'oeuvre (*gustatio*) could be simply prepared vegetables, eggs or fish, usually shellfish. The main course (*prima mensa*) included vegetables, meats (roast or boiled), sausages or rissoles, often sharply flavoured with herbs or liquamen. In one of Plautus' satires, in the third or second century BC, there are complaints that cooks season meals with condiments like screech owls, which eat the guests' intestines.

The last course (*secunda mensa*) might be of fruit, small cakes, or pastries sweetened with honey. Celsus, who wrote in the first century AD, warned that honeyed fruit was indigestible and a temptation to greed. Overindulgence was also a problem late in the evening. Wine could be drunk with the *secunda mensa* but was usually reserved for after the meal. Although the Romans professed themselves shocked at Celtic drinking habits, they were more concerned with the habit of drinking beer or wine undiluted than with the quantity consumed.

Food and the people

Food is always the first need which has to be satisfied. If supplies are scarce, people eat what they can to satisfy hunger. Tastes, however, become adaptable and people wish to try new commodities. The Romans increased the availability and variety of food in Britain, and plants acclimatized to their new habitat. The population probably ate reasonably well, especially on urban sites, where trade ensured a more varied diet than in the more remote parts of the west and north, where it would remain akin to that eaten in Iron Age Britain. That diet would be a diet of pottage made from ground legumes or cereals, which continued to be a peasant/rural diet for the next

1500 years. This diet, though high in fibre and protein, would lack certain vitamins, especially vitamin C, and might be somewhat debilitating. The want of a nutritious diet is shown in heights, as recorded on skeletal evidence. The average height of men seems to be 1.67m (5ft 6in) and of women 1.54m (5ft 1in), but this did not alter greatly until the improved nutrition of the mid-twentieth century. Although life in Roman Britain for some became more luxurious, for others it was a hard struggle for survival, dominated by anxiety when the crops failed.

Kitchens

In Celtic Britain the main cooking place had been the central hearth around which all the family gathered. This form of cooking certainly continued. Several female skeletons found in the Trentholme Drive cemetery at York showed evidence of squatting facets on the ankle bones, a feature of those who have spent much of their lives crouching by a fire or over a rotary quern. Towards the end of the Roman period, burnt patches on villa floors seem to indicate that the inhabitants reverted to cooking where they could rather than conventionally in a kitchen.

Chains found at Great Chesterford and Silchester were once attached to cauldrons used to boil joints of meat or to make pottage. A cauldron found at Prestwick Carr, Northumberland, had been patched continually as if the cook could not bear to throw it away. In the end it was deposited in a boggy area, a loved possession dedicated to a water deity. Some households might have followed the primitive method of using pot-boilers, where stones were heated then placed in a trough of water. Modern experiments in a stone-lined pit at Ballyvourney proved that 454 litres (100 gallons) of water, brought to the boil in thirty-five minutes, cooked perfectly a leg of mutton, wrapped in straw to prevent it from getting dirty.

At Clementhorpe, York, a fourth-century house had a domed oven. Charcoal or other heating matter, placed into it, would be raked out at the correct temperature to put in bread or other food. The oven was then sealed so that cooking took place in the dry heat. By the side was a tiled hearth, which showed evidence of burning; similar hearths have been found elsewhere, especially in London and Verulamium, where one had been placed, at some risk, next to a wooden wall. A heated surface acts as a griddle or can support a gridiron. Seneca, commenting on a man baking bread says, 'He made bread, which was first baked in the warm ashes on a red hot tile, then ovens were invented and other apparatus which depends on heat for its use.'

More usual was a raised hearth set in one part of the kitchen (**55**). This, edged with a curb to hold in the charcoal, was at waist height so that cooking could be done in a normal standing position using a gridiron or an iron tripod to support the pans. A square or semicircular indentation in the front of the hearth was for wood storage.

Normally fires were banked up at night but untended they can be dangerous so some houses had an isolated kitchen, similar to one in the Folkestone villa in Kent. If the fire went out it could be rekindled with flint and tinder, or the nearest neighbour might supply a light. Kitchens might be warm, comfortable places in winter, smelling of spices, cooked food and the herbs hung up to dry; on a warm day they might be uncomfortably hot with a lingering stale smell. Roman writers speak of smoke blackening the beams, which could also flavour hams, sausages and bacon, possibly placed on a wickerwork frame, which Pliny the Elder describes as hanging from the rafters over the hearth. Barrels, baskets and pots would be piled on the floor.

Storage vessels

In some houses at Silchester, pots sunk into the ground acted as storage containers; one careful owner placed ashes raked from the fire into a large earthenware vessel. Other pots contained food debris, including lamb, chicken and, in one instance, the complete scales of a carp. At Poundbury, Dorchester, analysis suggested milk products, olive-oil, wine, fish-sauce, honey and fruit extracts. In one corner, a broken amphora

55 *A kitchen as it might have appeared in a house at Cirencester. On the floor is a rotary quern. On the wall hangs a cauldron chain.*

might serve as a urinal. The cleaning out of these pots would be one of the most tedious and revolting jobs in the household. At the Folkestone villa, the cook ignored the food remains, which were left scattered round the fire. The Park Street and Chalk (Kent) villas had cellars to store their goods. Here could be placed *dolia,* large pottery storage vessels, built up by hand, but having a capacity of 909 litres (200 gallons), or the smaller version (*seriae*) with a capacity of between 90 to 295 litres (20–65 gallons). Many of these were imported until British potteries began their manufacture.

Cooking implements

Most of the Roman cooking implements are similar to modern ones because once a tool has proved its worth it becomes functional to that end and need not alter its basic shape. Utensils include frying-pans, some with a folding handle, *paterae*, *patellae* and *patinae*. A hoard from the Newstead fort, in Tweeddale, contained seven bronze globular-shaped cooking vessels of various sizes together with the gridiron on which they were placed (**56**). Most cooks have favourite pans. Exsuperius and Oconea both dedicated tablets at Bath cursing the thieves who had stolen theirs.

Several handsome bronze pans, pierced with holes forming an elegant pattern, might be filled with ice through which wine was poured in order to cool it. Lead pans are also known which might account for some traces of lead found in the Cirencester skeletons; iron pans give traces of iron to the food cooked in them but this is regarded as beneficial because it can combat anaemia.

Earthenware or terracotta bowls were common (**57**), the most usual being a wide-mouthed olla. Pots, if left unglazed, soured with use. Rubbing

56 *Cooking was often done in pots placed on a gridiron heated underneath by charcoal.*

57 *A group of pottery found at Aldborough, North Yorkshire, includes a flagon, a mortarium with a pouring lip and a triple vase.*

with sand cleaned them, but the huge amount of broken pottery found on Roman sites shows that it was easier to throw them away. Sometimes a lime coating on the interior has been left by boiling water. Handmade shell-tempered storage jars found in London had pitch on the rims and shoulders, indicating that they had been sealed, possibly to preserve salt prepared along the Thames Estuary. Amphorae provide excellent containers. One at Silchester had the word *Aven(a)* (oats) written on it. Pottery jars were sealed with wooden or

58 *The great circular silver dish, centre-piece of a hoard of thirty-four pieces of silver found at Mildenhall in Suffolk. In the centre is a mask of Oceanus, with dolphins intertwined in his hair.*

clay stoppers, or were covered with an inverted jar. Some pottery vessels were obviously strainers, perhaps for honey or soft cheese but more delicate straining would be done through fine cloth. Bases of cheese-presses have been found at Colchester, York, Wroxeter and Richborough.

Polae for pounding herbs and spices were common. Food could be pulverized in mortaria, essential when vegetables were more fibrous. A mortarium of second-century date, found at Silchester, had the remains of pulped fruit stones and pips in it. Vessels, up to 90cm (36in) in diameter, often had large spouts allowing easy pouring. Lion-headed spouts decorated Lezoux pottery imported through London; imports from the Eifel region of the Rhineland were of a coarse stone-like, pimply material.

Other kitchen implements included cleavers, knives of all kinds, spoons and flesh-hooks. The Romans also knew the use of the bain-marie and water heaters, though none is known in Britain. A portable metal or earthenware oven was also used to keep dishes hot at the table. Steelyards had weights in the form of heads, which often represent a deity. Roman recipes give weight in the form of *librae* (pounds), *unciae* (ounces) and *scrupuli* (scruples). Five raised dots indicated a weight of five *unciae* at Colchester; one at Glenlocher had *s(emis)*, that is, half a *libra* or six *unciae*, scratched on to it. Few correspond to the exact weight; most are under the marked measurement. Standard weights and measures, against which discrepancies could be checked, are known to have existed in Rome. But experienced cooks do not use exact measurements; few are given in Apicius' cookery book.

Tableware

More sophisticated vessels, used to grace the dining-table rather than act as kitchenware, would be made of Nene valley, New Forest and Oxfordshire ware. *Bibe* (Drink well!) instructed some beakers imported from the Rhineland, decorated with trailed barbotine or depicting hunting scenes, where the fluidity of movement delighted the former British aristocracy. People swiftly adopt implements which are more practical, hygienic or enable them to indulge personal preferences. These included glassware of all forms for both storage and serving of food, and silver and bronze plate and vessels. Silverware such as the Mildenhall Treasure, too valuable to use for eating purposes, made an attractive and valuable decoration (**58**). Pewter vessels appeared in the fourth century. A tableservice found in a well at Appleshaw, Hampshire, was probably dumped there by its owner in an attempt to save it from thieves.

6
Personal life-style

Iron Age clothing

Surviving descriptions of Celtic dress, especially in the Irish texts, suggest a love of colourful fashion. Cu Chulainn rode to woo Emer wearing a crimson tunic, long-sleeved and fastened at the breast with a salmon brooch, covered with a white hooded shirt, interwoven red with flaming gold. Over his left shoulder he bore a crimson-coloured shield edged with silver and chased with golden animal figures; at his waist was a golden-hilted sword and in his right hand he held a silver spear. Similar dress was worn by the Gauls, of whom Diodorus remarks that, 'They wear tunics which have been dyed and embroidered . . . and striped cloaks fastened by a brooch on the shoulder.' Tunics were also made of leather. Pigskin is both supple and long-lasting, and the large amount of pork consumed would ensure an availability of skins.

Trousers are mentioned in the Irish texts, but Strabo and Diodorus comment that the continental Celts wore breeches. Tight breeches are worn by a horned figure on the Gundestrup cauldron, deposited in a Danish bog and now in the National Museum in Copenhagen, who is clothed in a V-necked, long-sleeved one-piece garment of heavy rib pattern, reaching only to the knees and held in place by an embroidered or metal-encrusted belt. Breeches are worn by the accompanying procession of warriors, but some riders wear short tunics and long trousers, wider at the ankles and not gripping the leg. It was the wearing of trousers and breeches which distin-

guished the men of northern Europe from those in the southern areas. They were the practical garments of a horse-riding people, originating in the steppes of central Europe. Certainly they were more suitable for the colder weather in the north.

Celtic women loved decorative garments. When Eochaid Airem wooed Etain, 'whose hair seemed like red-gold after the burnishing', she wore a long tunic, ornamented with a silver fringe and a long purple cloak decorated with golden embroidery, held in place by a gold brooch. Eochaid noted teeth like a shower of pearls, cheeks red as the foxglove, eyebrows dark as a stag beetle and lips red as rowan berries. Presumably Etain was not averse to art helping out nature. Eyebrows could be dyed with berry juice and cheeks reddened with a herb called ruan.

Not all Celtic women were attractive. Dornoll, the daughter of Domnall, who trained Cu Chulainn in feats of arms, had a face as black as a bowl of jet, a large forehead and rough bright-red hair in threads woven round her head. Her nickname of 'Big-fist' indicates the size of her hands. Not surprisingly, Cu Chulainn recoiled from her at first glance. Ammianus Marcellinus commented that a whole host of foreigners could not withstand a single Gaul if he called to his aid his wife, 'who is usually very strong, gnashing her teeth and brandishing her sallow arms of enormous size', especially when she struck 'blows mingled with kicks as if they were so many missiles from a string of catapults'.

Both men and women wore cloaks. Diodorus comments that they 'were striped, heavy for winter wear and light for summer, in which are set checks close together'. This description of a kind of plaid is confirmed by Pliny the Elder's comment that the Gauls introduced check patterns. Cloaks of Irish chieftains were five-folded, to provide a heavy warm garment. Strabo mentions that the Gauls wove thick cloaks from a wool which was tough but thin at the ends. By pressing the thread of the weave close together a kind of Harris tweed would result, eminently suitable for keeping out the rain.

A love of jewellery accompanied brightly coloured clothes. Strabo said that the Gauls wore ornaments of gold, torcs on their necks and bracelets on their arms, while people of high rank wore dyed garments besprinkled with gold. Jewellery found in pre-Roman graves in both Britain and Gaul includes anklets, bracelets and pendants. In Dorset craftsmen took advantage of local material to produce shale bracelets. Necklaces of glass, bone and amber are not uncommon.

Changes of style in Roman Britain

This love of brightly coloured dress would no doubt have continued during the early years of Roman Britain. But women are attracted by new fashions and men also follow what is now called power-dressing, often to make a political statement. Both would adopt Roman dress, which was designed on more sober lines in keeping with the dignity of Roman authority. Women would also be expected to take a subservient role. On a tombstone at Chester, Marcus Aurelius Nepos carries a centurion's stick; his wife has a distaff and weaving comb, indicating her duty to see that slaves or the female members of the family spun and wove cloth, although this could be bought in the shops or from travelling salesmen.

Textile fragments found in Britain include plain weave, herringbone and diamond twills, and a half-basket weave. Linen has been found but silk and damask are rare; silk was, however,

found in the child's grave at Holborough. One piece of cotton came from a well at Chew Stoke (Avon) but, although known to the Romans, the material was rarely used. Wool was the most common material for garments. There would be no problem with dyeing of garments, which could be as brightly coloured as those worn by the Celts. Textile pieces found are purple, russet brown, black and yellow. Evidence from York suggests that purple was obtained by soaking in a mixture of lichen and urine. Woad provided shades of blue, and weld produced yellow.

Breeches and trousers probably survived in country areas, especially in the north where practical considerations prevailed, but anyone taking part in public life had to abandon Celtic ways. No doubt the sons of the nobility were told firmly that breeches were part of a barbaric culture and incompatible with civilized life, so that their wearing soon became archaic. However, Roman legionaries did wear some form of knee breeches; auxiliaries, who were allowed to wear their native dress, often wore them.

Tunics

The basic Roman dress consisted of a tunic, which hung loose or was belted at the waist to produce an overfold. Under a short tunic, draped to fall to the knees, a man probably worn a tunic undergarment and perhaps a loincloth or a pair of drawers. Textile remains indicate colourful garments although the Romans often preferred plain, unbleached woollen ones, with a coloured band around the hem or the sleeves. Sometimes tunics were tied over one shoulder. Smiths portrayed at York (**59**) and Corbridge (**60**) wear one like this for ease and convenience: it leaves one arm free and would be cool in the heat of the forge.

Three pairs of leather briefs have been found in London but these were probably worn by athletes; it would be more comfortable to wear linen or woollen ones. During menstruation women could pad themselves with a loincloth tied with cords. Fasteners could include small hooks but more probably reliance was placed on strips of cloth or leather. Strips of cloth could flatten a bust or, carefully arranged, emphasize it.

Women wore a long stola and under this a long shift. On one tombstone, Curatia Dinysia lolls in an almost tipsy fashion, cup in right hand, wearing a light tunic gathered at the hips in a bunched knot and arranged so as to cling to the legs.

On her tombstone, Julia Velva lies on a couch attended by her heir, Mercurialis, and her female attendant (**61**). All wear tunics; that of Mercurialis is short whereas both the women

59 *The smith on a relief at York wears a tunic fastened over one shoulder.*

60 *A smith on a plaque found at Corbridge, near Hadrian's Wall. This portrayal, like that of the smith from York, has been suggested as the Celtic smith god who syncretized his activities with those of Vulcan.*

61 *The tombstone of Julia Velva at York. Her heir, L. Aurelius Mercurialis, who set up the tombstone, wears a thick, 'Gallic coat' with tightly fitted sleeves, over which is a warm mantle. Stout boots keep his feet warm.*

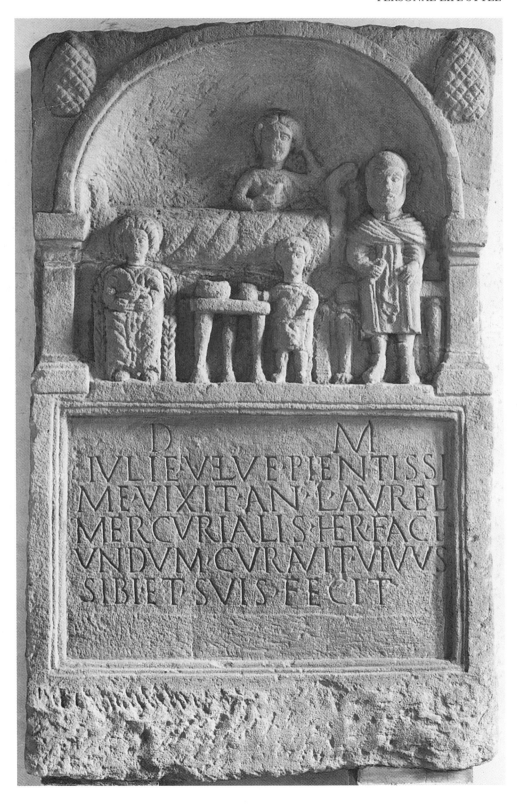

62 *Gaius Aeresius Saenus, a veteran of the Sixth Legion, set up this tombstone at York to his 'beloved wife', Flavia Augustina, who died aged 39. Both her children, although their appearance suggests they lived several years, died before they reached the age of two.*

wear long ones. The attendant's is amply gathered in folds round the waist. Mercurialis has a thick cloak flung around him as if he feels the cold. On another funerary relief at York, Victor, a freedman, wears a long tunic, V-shaped at the neck, with three-quarter-length sleeves. Over this is thrown a long strip of material which serves as a shawl. A little boy, holding up a wine cup, wears his short tunic arranged blouson-style; the bare minimum of his clothing suggests a lower status. A somewhat similar garment to Victor's is worn by Barates' wife, Regina. Her long-sleeved tunic falls in heavy folds with ample material in the sleeves. This garment, called the Gallic coat, worn by both men and women, was suitable for the cold northern areas.

Even more elaborate is the garment worn by the woman depicted on the Murrell Hill tombstone. The fashionable effect lies in the mantle draped over the shoulder; this leaves her right hand free to grasp a huge circular fan, which, judging by its prominent position in the carving, was a cherished possession. The ivory sticks of a fan of similar design were found placed with its owner in her sarcophagus in York.

Warm clothing

The cold winds of York had blown around the family of Flavia Augustina, wife of Gaius Aeresius, a veteran of the Sixth Legion (**62**). They and their two children are dressed in thick Gallic cloaks, sleeves down to the wrists and heavy voluminous folds forming a stylish V-shape in front. The tombstone of Julia Brica and her daughter, Sempronia Martina, also from York, shows similar garments. An even heavier cloak clothes the figure of a seated mother goddess at Bewcastle (Cumbria). Seemingly worn over a long tunic, its voluminous sleeves give the impression of a comfortable, warm, loose garment.

Thick garments seen on figures elsewhere on tombstones at Chester and Caerleon and draping the stern figures of the mother goddesses at Cirencester reinforce the impression that warm clothing was essential to Britain. The army realized this, as the relief of the *optio*, Caecilus Avitus (**63**), indicates, because the heavy cloak is drawn tightly together at the front. The mason has hacked it roughly to indicate tough woollen fibres.

63 *Caecilus Avitus as portrayed on his tombstone at Chester wears a heavy cloak, which the mason has hacked roughly to indicate tough woollen fibres.*

Cloaks

Cloaks shown on reliefs are placed over the head, put round the shoulders or wound round the neck with the ends thrown back. One imitated the Celtic garb of the *cucullus* which ploughmen found useful, as the small figurine from Piercebridge indicates (**64**). This garment had a cult status, representing the *Genii Cucullati,* and the detailed carving from Housesteads shows cloaks falling to just above the ankles. The edges of the garments are thickened as if there was a double fold here. No fastenings are shown but they were probably held together by brooches. The *cucullus* was a hood which widened into a cape.

A longer cloak was a *byrrus* which had a hood attached (**65**). One is worn by Philus on his tombstone at Gloucester. Diocletian's edict of AD 301 mentions cloaks of several qualities including a *Britannicus* one worth 6000 denarii. The dearest one, the Nervian, made in Gaul, was 10,000 denarii, while the cheapest, costing 1500, was of North African manufacture. Cloaks, eminently suitable for wet weather, could also be made of skins and leather.

Curse tablets from Bath suggest that cloaks were such desirable garments that they were often stolen. There were no lockers in the baths; bathers should tip a slave or an attendant to look after their clothes. At least seven cloaks went missing and Solinus would have found himself in a most embarrassing situation, when both his

64 *Bronze figurine of a ploughman found at Piercebridge, County Durham, showing him wearing a* cucullus, *possibly made of leather.*

65 *Philus who died near Cirencester wears a* byrrus, *a long heavy cloak of fine wool to which a hood was attached. As Philus originally came from the tribe of the Sequani, who lived in the Upper Saône valley in Gaul, he might have purchased his expensive-looking cloak there.*

cloak and his bathing tunic, a garment worn under the cloak when leaving the baths, were stolen.

The toga

The garments described above could have been worn equally by anyone in Roman Britain having Celtic or Roman views. The Roman garment, the toga, was a different matter. The wearer of such a garment indicated that he, for it was worn only by men, had accepted an office of importance. Tacitus remarks that in the second winter of his governorship (AD 79), Agricola's policy of Romanization was so successful that the British determined to learn Latin and the toga was everywhere to be seen, flaunted, no doubt, by young bloods determined to be in the new fashion.

The toga was a difficult garment to wear, being a huge semicircular piece of material 5.6m (8½ft) long and 2.13m (7ft) across at its widest point (**66**). Magistrates and youths under sixteen wore one with a scarlet or purple stripe along the straight edge; mourners wore one of black or a dark colour. Candidates seeking office indicated their intention by wearing one of bleached white; otherwise it was made of unbleached natural wool.

The arrangement of this garment was complicated for it had to be placed over the left shoulder and arm, taken under the right arm, and then over the head, finally being gathered and twisted in front to hold it. It required skill to make the drapery fall easily and as the weight was considerable men had to walk slowly and with dignity, which prevented any rash movement, particularly where weapons were concerned. In Rome it was often regarded as such a nuisance to wear that the emperors were compelled to issue edicts for its wearing on formal occasions. In Britain, its adoption in the first

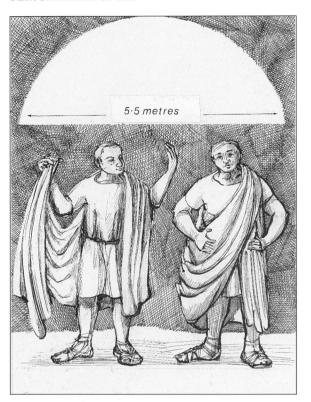

66 *Wearing the Roman toga.*

longitudinal strap on the top of the foot joining with an ankle strap (**67**). Shoemaking was a professional craft, where both soles and uppers were carefully cut from waste pieces of cattle hide or goatskin. Sandals might be made for each customer by tracing around the sole of the foot. If so, one of the earliest cases of bunions has come to light, as a sandal from London has revealed that the owner's toes were out of joint; two other shoes had been made for someone with a clubbed foot.

Light sandals were worn indoors; their owners could kick them off when reclining at table. For outer wear nailed shoes and boots were worn, often made from layers of leather which gave greater protection. They might have a closed upper, seamed from the opening to the toes with a series of large thonged holes. By the mid-second century a latchet shoe had become popular, with an openwork upper.

Ladies had more choice with a slipper form of shoe. A pair taken by one lady to her grave at Southfleet (Kent) was of dark blue leather enhanced by hexagonal cutouts, outlined with

67 *A sandal found in London.*

century would outwardly indicate enthusiasm for the new regime as well as presenting to the world a visible sign of sharing power with the elite.

It is difficult to find a representation of anyone wearing a toga in Britain. On the marble sarcophagus of Gaius Etruscus from London is a roundel depicting the upper part of a man wearing a toga. This was an imported piece with a stereotyped carving on it. Nevertheless Gaius may have selected this receptacle for himself in death because he was proud to have worn the toga in life.

Footwear

The Celts had worn footwear of hide, although many had gone barefoot. A moccasin type, made of one piece of skin and tied with thongs, was also worn by the Romans. In the third century women's styles became narrower and men's wider. Sandals were fastened by thongs around the toes, especially the big toe, or with a gold thonging. A shoe found in London had expensive gold-leaf decoration with a cork sole. Another, at Vindolanda, had a wooden sole with a thick leather strap to hold it on, a type of shoe recommended today to ensure healthy feet.

Jewellery

Cloaks were fastened, as they had been in pre-Roman Britain, with brooches. The choice widened considerably. There were fibulae like safety-pins, or ones, with a humorous touch, designed as tortoises, hares, dolphins and, a popular design in the East Anglian region, riders on horseback. A swastika brooch from Brough-on-Humber would also serve as an amulet bringing good luck. A direct result of the fusion between Celtic and Roman traditions in the first century AD produced the dragonesque brooches found in the northern areas (**68**). Trumpet fibulae also combined Celtic enamelling with the Roman skill in silverwork. Craftsmen continued to produce the torc. Regina wears one on her tombstone at South Shields but she may have been sentimental about her Catuvellaunian origins or have inherited an heirloom. Necklaces seem to have been popular; one from Richborough interlinked gold and sapphires, and heavy gold chains were found on sites along Hadrian's Wall. Many necklaces included an amulet of a crescent or a spoked wheel.

From her trinket box, which might be locked with a special key worn as a finger-ring, a woman could take necklaces of gold, bone, amber, jet, coral, pottery and shell, bracelets, earrings and rings. Craftsmen in York and Malton, using jet from the outcrops at Whitby, or jewellers in Dorset using the local shale, could supply her wants. Serpent jewellery associated with the underworld and death, with Bacchus and good luck, with Aesculapius and healing, was popular. A hoard hidden at Snettisham (Norfolk) during the second century included rings and bracelets.

Rings, rare in pre-Roman Britain, adorned hands – every finger if required, many set with precious stones or intaglios, carved with a huge variety of devices and figures to suit every taste (**colour plate 9**). The chosen device, when

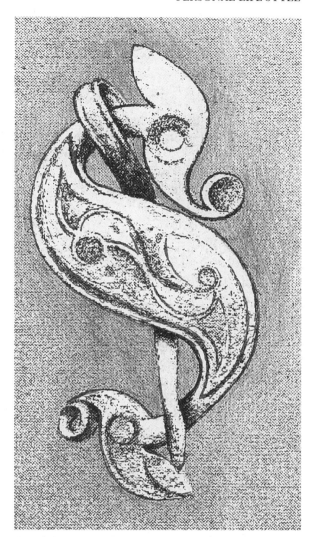

68 *A dragonesque brooch.*

stamped into wax, would be a seal giving a document the force of law. A woman, for sentimental reasons, might prefer carvings of Venus or Cupid, while men wanted Victory or Mars. One found near Bedford, inscribed *Eusebia Vita* (life to Eusebia), seems to be a love token. Women living near Carlisle could buy gems from a workshop recently identified as being in that area. Crucibles found at Cirencester and Verulamium indicate that gold- or silversmiths set up shops there. At Norton near Malton the slave who had the opportunity to manage a goldsmith's shop supplied customers' needs.

69 *Hairpins found at Aldborough reveal several styles.*

Itinerant jewellers would travel the land. One either lost or deliberately deposited his gems in the waters of Bath. Another deposited his total stock at Thetford, a hoard of eighty-three pieces of gold and silver buried for safety and never regained. No doubt husbands were willing to buy jewellery, because conspicuous display on a woman showed their wealth. Regina holds the domestic implements of distaff and spindle on her tombstone, but her jewel box is also prominently displayed. Women took their jewel boxes to the grave with them as did one lady at York, whose wooden box containing jet jewellery and perfume bottles was securely locked. Brooches fastened shrouds, and personal ornaments were set by the body (**69**), some bent or broken to allow their life spirit to accompany their owner beyond the grave. With the coming of Christianity, although such practices declined, the dead refused to be parted from their jewellery, either for sentimental reasons or for reassurance in the next world.

Accessories

Accessories included fans, and if the evidence from a grave at York has been correctly interpreted, a parasol. A leather purse was found at Holborough and a linen one at Husthwaite in North Yorkshire; a lady on a tombstone from Chester appears to be holding a clutch bag. Bronze arm purses, like the one found at Birdoswald, are believed to have been worn only by the military. The Romans did not usually wear gloves, although leather ones would protect the hands while using heavy tools. The Elder Pliny's secretary protected his hands with long sleeves when he was reading during bitterly cold weather. But, on a curse tablet from Bath, Docimedis asks that the person who has stolen his two gloves should lose his minds (*sic*) and his eyes.

Beards and hairstyles

Both women and men wished to make themselves attractive to the other sex and in so doing suffered in the process. In the last years of the republic and the early years of the empire men were clean-shaven. If a slave did not shave him a man would go to one of the numerous barbers' shops, which also acted as social meeting-places, for the barber, then as now, was the collector and dispenser of gossip. Diocletian's price edict says that a shave should cost no more than two sesterces, probably worth that for the information which could be gained. A sharp knife or a *novacula,* which may be a form of rough razor, had to be held by an expert. The blade scraped the face, well-softened beforehand for the Romans did not use soap.

A good barber was one to be treasured. Cuts were so frequent that a list of damages was drawn up. Martial warned men to avoid the barber Antiocus, who had inflicted scars without number on his chin. Pliny the Elder gave a recipe for a plaster made from spiders' webs mixed with oil and vinegar to staunch the blood. Some men had their hairs plucked out one by one and, to quote Martial again, 'Part of your jaw is clipped, part is shaved, part is plucked of hair. Who would imagine this to be a single head?'

It was the Emperor Hadrian who brought in the beard as a fashion. His biographer said that he wished to hide a scar on his chin but his decision was probably followed with relief. His portrait on coins and on statues, such as the one found in London, together with his personal visit in AD 122 would have encouraged the fashion.

Hair was dressed according to the fashion of the current emperor and until the second century was a simple back and sides. Certainly in Britain the Celtic fashion of dressing it with limewater would lose favour. Roman writers refer to a comb, scissors, which seem to be two strips of sharpened metal, and a *calamist,* which may be a curling iron. Martial mentions putting dye on the hair and perfume on the face; some men even wore patches to hide blemishes.

Women's hairstyles

Celtic women had worn their hair loose. Boudicca, according to Diodorus, presented a powerful vision, 'huge of frame, terrifying in all aspects ... and with a great mane of red hair falling to her knees'. Fedhelm, a prophetess mentioned in the Irish tales, had long golden hair. Three tresses were wound round her head, another fell down her back to reach her calves. On a relief at Ilkley (W. Yorks.) a woman has two long tresses dangling in front of her. If flung over her back they would have reached to the waist. Aurelia Aureliana from Carlisle has her hair hanging at least to her shoulders and possibly down her back. Venus, on a relief from High Rochester, Northumberland, grips her hair in two thick bunches.

In the first century the elaborate hairstyle of the Flavian dynasty is revealed on a portrait bust at Bath; ridges of tight curls outline the forehead, while the rest of the hair is drawn back in a bun. Such an elaborate hairstyle demands the attention of an attendant as does that on an actual head of hair found preserved in a grave at York, where the centre piece is plaited, drawn back from the forehead and wrapped round the head (**70**); another plaited piece rises directly from the forehead to be pulled back across the top of the head. On the Neumagen relief one attendant draws the hair into a bun; two others stand ready with perfumes and oils to anoint the hair and keep it in place. If false hair was required, it could, as Martial mentions, be taken from captive slaves. Women might also have sold their hair as they continued to do throughout the centuries.

Julia Velva and her daughter have a simple style, with a centre parting and a bun at the back; another style has the bun on top of the head, as worn by a lady on a relief found at Halton Chesters on Hadrian's Wall. In the early third

70 *Hair twisted into a bun and held in place by jet pins survived on the body of a woman found in the Railway cemetery, York.*

century a visit to Britain by the Empress Julia Domna possibly caused hairstyles to be dressed in the Syrian fashion with crimped hair on either side of the head. Volusia Faustina, the wife of a decurion at Lincoln, might have felt she was in the height of fashion and also bringing honour to her husband by copying the empress.

Painting the face

After the hair the face would require attention. Ovid, in his poem 'Painting the Face' (at the end of the first century BC), gives details for Roman women, but as he began with a facepack of ten eggs, two pounds of vetch, two pounds of skimmed barley, twelve pounded narcissus bulbs, gum, pounded Tuscan seed and one and a half pounds of honey, few Romano-British women might have used it. More practical was a toner made from poppies pounded with water. His recommended facepack of honey, egg and oatmeal could be applied today. Ovid suggests a remedy for getting rid of spots but says bluntly, cover them with small patches or powder.

Scent was applied liberally. Many scents and perfumes were imported in small globular-shaped bottles or in flasks, often created in bizarre shapes, like the small bald-headed figure found at

York (**71**); others were of intricate workmanship like the tired slave found at Aldborough. The contents of a small flagon, recently discovered in the Hunsrück region of Germany, have been analysed as a mixture of animal fat, sandalwood and lavender, a concoction clearly intended as a beauty cream. Some beauty aids were lethal: white lead for cheeks and powdered antimony for eyebrows would destroy rather than enhance beauty. Juvenal's suggestion of soot for eyebrows would have been embarrassing for anyone going out into the rain!

Toilet articles

Sets of toilet articles or chatelaines consisting of earpicks and scoops, scrapers and tweezers were essential equipment. Hair on legs and armpits was plucked out or rubbed with pumice. Pliny the Elder suggests a depilatory cream made from the blood of a wild she-goat mixed with sea palm or powdered viper's gall. Women suffered a great

71 *A balsamarium from York in the shape of a bald-headed child. Many of these grotesque figures were made at Alexandria in Egypt and were exported throughout the empire.*

deal to make themselves attractive but men also shared their pain for the sake of fashion.

The final effect would be viewed in a mirror. The most ornate is a circular silver pocket one found at Wroxeter and its weight is such that it must have been held by an attendant. Celtic women had viewed themselves in polished bronze mirrors like those found at Birdlip (Glos.) and Desborough (Northants), decorated with intricate incised or enamelled decoration on the back. The figure assumed to be Venus or a fertility deity on the Rudston mosaic is so overcome by what she sees in her mirror that she drops it. Glass mirrors were found at Reculver (Kent) and York, and square lead frames, which would have held glass, were found at Chester and Ospringe (Kent). A Chester tombstone shows a lady standing pensively holding a comb in one hand and a mirror with a knobbed handle in the other. Her maid accompanies her carrying the tray on which the toilet articles rest. Thoughtfully they assess the final effect, re-enacting in death a scene which had been repeated so often in life.

Hygienic water supplies

Good health, to some extent, depends upon sanitary conditions. After the conquest copious supplies of fresh water were brought to even the smallest town, often by means of an open conduit. A nearby spring was tapped where possible, but at Lincoln an elaborate arrangement of terracotta pipes sheathed in concrete conveyed water over 32km (20 miles); one pipeline supplied the baths, the other water for public use. Wroxeter was provided with 9 million litres (2 million gallons) a day and even a small town such as Dorchester brought water from a source 19km (12 miles) distance. Wooden pipes were usual; lead pipes were found at Bath and some military sites, such as at York. Vitruvius remarks that public money should supply fountains, cisterns and baths. Private customers had to pay for water supplied to their homes and some households at Catterick were prepared to do this.

The primary purpose of the public water supply was to feed the bath establishments. Water also flowed into collecting points but because it loses its freshness when brought along the open leat, aerating in some form was necessary, often by cascading from one tank to another. As the water was delivered on the constant-flow principle, the surplus was removed by drains or soakaways.

For drinking water many towns were dependent on wells; London had a vast number. A well might be partly used as a cesspit or dug next to one so that seepage occurred. Pliny the Elder warned that water should issue from the bottom not the side of wells and the practice of lining wells with stone, timber or basketwork indicates that this was done. Farms and villas could use a convenient water supply. The owners of the Chedworth villa collected their water from the spring line in an elaborate nymphaeum; rainwater was also collected.

Drainage and sewerage

At London a series of drains arranged to cover the waterfront terraces were kept clear until the fourth century. In some towns drainage and sewerage systems were the same: York, Lincoln and Colchester benefited from this attention; other towns, such as Winchester and Chichester, had roadside gullies to remove surplus water. William Stukeley, the eighteenth-century antiquary, commented that at Chester the drains were so high that a man could walk upright along the whole length, and at York the main sewer was large enough for any blockage to be cleaned by slaves who could enter through manholes. Yet this sewer, which collected water from the baths, the streets and presumably from latrines, debouched into the tidal River Foss. The York drains were constructed of rough-hewn blocks of stone; those at Colchester were lined with pink mortar. Both might allow faeces to cling to them but the constant water flow could dilute the solid sewage thus preventing too great an odour. For most towns, however, as at Silchester, the only drainage would be an open sewer.

There might be public latrines. At Verulamium one enterprising householder provided a latrine

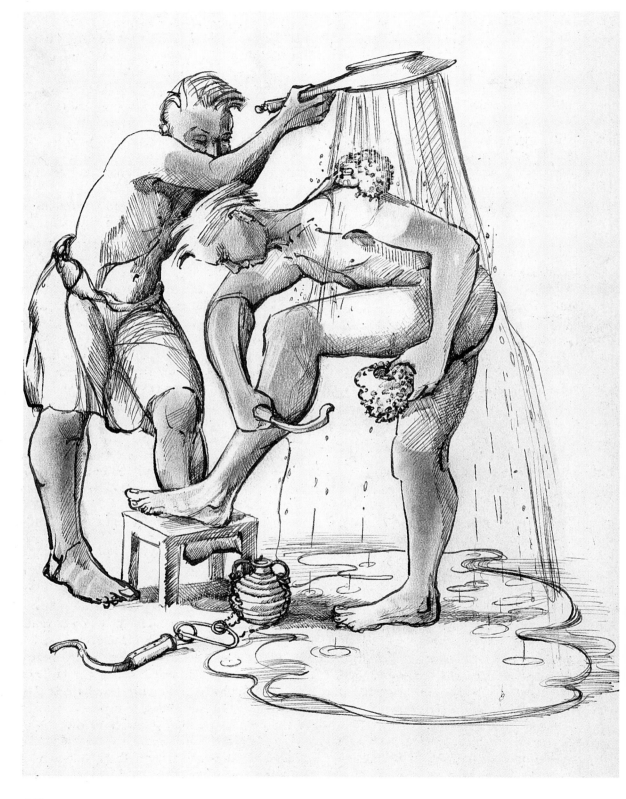

72 A man scrapes himself with a strigil. By his feet is a small oil flask.

accessible from the street. Large bath systems, as at London and Bath, would have had them as a matter of course, usually in the form of wooden or stone seats over a deep trench, as has been suggested at the Housesteads fort (**colour plate 10**). Moss, or a sponge on a stick, was used as toilet paper; pieces of sponge were found in the York sewers. The practice of using communal sponges would have little to commend it especially as they were washed in water running along an open gutter. Many people carried their own sponge, which came in handy for one gladiator, whom, as Martial recounts, rather than fight the wild beasts in the arena, committed suicide by stuffing the stick down his throat.

Household latrines were built over cesspits, their contents piling up until removed by slaves or sold as fertilizer. Amphorae, placed strategically at street corners, served a double purpose as the urine collected could be used in tanneries. At Pompeii householders put notices on the wall warning people not to use the street as a toilet — *Cave malam* (You'll be sorry!).

Bathing establishments

Bathing establishments were automatically attached to forts; villa builders included them and in the fourth century many owners enlarged them or provided a separate bath-house. In the towns their establishment was a popular part of the benefits of civilization. Tacitus had included them among his amenities that made vice agreeable. The first-century complex at Huggin Hill in London is contemporary with those at Silchester and Bath. Available to all, either freely or for a modest fee, baths were warm, comfortable places, open all day and constantly in use. Mixed or separate bathing for the sexes took place and the baths had a social as well as a cleansing function (**colour plate 11**).

Visitors went from the outer gymnasium to the undressing-room, leaving clothes in niches or cupboards or paying someone to keep a watch on

them; reference has already been made to the problems at Bath. There was a large cold bath for those brave enough to plunge in, or a small basin of water for sprinkling. Bathers moved to the warm room, then plunged into the hot water bath or sweated in a hotter, drier temperature, where a slave could scrape off the dirt and moisture with a strigil (**72**). The route was reversed ending with a dip in the water to close the pores, especially necessary in Britain to prevent the bather getting a chill.

Fragments of glass, discovered in bath-houses, were once bottles containing perfumes and oils, possibly for aromatherapy. Tweezers, earpicks and nail-cleaners suggest manicures; hair-plucking and ear-clearing were provided. Shellfish debris, mutton chops and chicken bones found in the Caerleon legionary baths indicate that snack-bars were part of the amenities offered. Chatting to friends, gossiping and relaxing would contribute towards mental health; advice could be sought on health and dietetics. But Seneca, who lived above one in Rome, thought they were noisy places. He was disturbed by 'shouts, grunts, slaps ... and the screams of those who were having their armpits plucked'. Nevertheless exercising of limbs under water eases strains and aching muscles. The Roman bathing establishments made a contribution to what today is called community health.

There was also a spiritual dimension. Baths were associated with healing, which was a gift from the gods. Bath and Lydney Park (Glos.), as healing cult sanctuaries, were arranged on the same lines as others throughout the empire. Bath, in particular, still has over a million litres (250,000 gallons) a day bubbling up at a constant temperature of 48°C (120°F). Under the auspices of Sulis Minerva the complex of temple, theatre and healing shrine attracted soldiers and civilians in search of physical and spiritual well-being (**73**). A life-size gilded head of the goddess displays a dignified appearance reassuring to those who sought her aid. Numerous votive offerings, the majority of them coins, testify the appreciation of those who were cured, or, equally important, felt

73 *Complex at Bath showing baths, theatre, courtyard and altar. (Drawing by Alan Sorrell)*

themselves to be cured. Some, such as the son of Novantius, were so affected by the atmosphere that they experienced visions.

Lydney Park healing sanctuary was dedicated to the Celtic god Nodens. On two bronze votive plaques he is associated with Mars whom, as well as being a warrior god, is also linked to healing. The temple, a basilican-type building, together with a guest-house, was set around a colonnaded court and a huge suite of baths. Votive offerings found here include an engraved bone plaque showing a woman pressing her hands against her stomach, an obvious reference to childbirth.

There are also several bronze models of dogs. The dog, connected with the Celtic underworld as guardian and guide, was often encouraged to lick sores and wounds in the hope of effecting a cure.

One interpretation of the inscription on a mosaic floor, laid not later than AD 367, suggested that it was dedicated by T. Flavius Senilis, superintendent of religious rites, who financed it from offerings. He was given assistance by Victorinus, an interpreter of dreams. Possibly some form of drug-induced or ritual sleep was part of the healing process; hence the necessity of providing guest-rooms in this isolated area.

Bathing establishments, therefore, contributed to both mental and physical welfare but there were problems. The large latrines, allowing sewage to be concentrated in one area, would debouch into the nearest river. Unless the authorities constantly changed the water or added some disinfecting substance, infection might be rife in the warm pools. The Romans had no concept of disease-carrying organisms and the arrangement for drinking water depended more on reaction to fresh- or foul-tasting water than a knowledge of health. The perils of drinking impure water are underlined by the discovery at Orton Longueville (Cambs.), in a woman's skeleton, of a calcified hydatid cyst, the size of a chicken's egg, caused by a tapeworm which had found its way into the lung. Death was probably caused by the bursting of the abscess.

Diseases of the eye

Bathing establishments could induce people to follow a fitness regime but bad health was a problem, especially diseases affecting eyesight. Trachoma caused by a virus prevalent in unhygienic conditions and carried by flies, would be common. Failing sight can be due to lack of vitamin C or vitamin A. Both these are to be found in green vegetables, which were lacking in the winter, but vitamin A is also found in animal fats especially in liver. At Wroxeter a pair of sheet-gold eyes and over thirty eyes cut out of wallplaster suggest desperately given votive offerings by people in search of a cure.

Bath and Lydney have provided some of the examples of oculist stamps, small four-sided tablets on which are carved retrograde inscriptions. These could be pressed on to a dried ointment cake or stick, or on to small pottery vessels, holding eye-salve. Valerius Amandus advertised vinegar ointment for running eyes and a celandine salve as a cure for inflammation. At Cirencester, Attius advised poppy salve; Tiberius Claudius recommended frankincense salve for all eye trouble and at Bath T. Junianus made his somewhat rash claim that his quince salve for clearing the vision was for *any* medical defect. The prescription of Julius Jucundus at Lydney gave three different ways of using it: in drops, as an ointment mixed with quince-oil or as a tincture to be applied with a sponge.

Salves and ointments

Pure honey applied to a cut to stem bleeding and keep the wound clear was a cure used down to this century. Balsam (balm) can be any form of ointment, but it also means opobalsamum – an exuded resin from trees in the Near East. As well as on the eyes, it was used for wounds, for arthritis or even internally. Another ointment was Lycium, which came from Asia Minor, but a variety from India was highly regarded in the treatment of eye disease. A substance similar to this was found in a pot in a grave at Weston Turville, and Michael Faraday's analysis of a substance on basketwork in one of the Bartlow Hills' barrows suggested that it was myrrh or frankincense.

Skeletal evidence

Skeletal evidence produces a sobering picture. Evidence from Cirencester led the excavators to suggest that at least 80 per cent of the adult population had osteoarthritis, while at Dorchester-on-Thames, in a cemetery in use from the late fourth to the early sixth century, almost everyone over the age of thirty was affected by osteoarthritis in the spine. A large number of bones in all the cemeteries showed wear and tear on the joints, or bone fractures caused by accidents at work, a misdirected hammer blow perhaps, or a slip in ploughing. Some of the bones showed evidence of tuberculosis, others of poliomyelitis.

Surprisingly at Cirencester, Ilchester (Som.) and York the teeth were in good condition with little evidence of dental caries. This would not be due to oral hygiene but to a lack of sweet foods in the diet or perhaps to the fluoride occurring in the water. A high-fibre diet also protects the teeth because it adheres to them less than does highly refined foods. But excavations at Baldock show the population there suffered from bad teeth.

Few people at Cirencester had lived beyond their early forties; at Dorchester-on-Thames only 50 per cent of the men and 30 per cent of the women survived the age of forty. This seems better than at Lankhills cemetery, Winchester, where only 52 of 248 skeletons examined indicated survival beyond the age of thirty. The average age of death at Ilchester was 40 for men, 36 for women, while at Vindolanda the average dropped to 28 for women. Many women probably died in childbirth or from puerperal fever. The overwhelming feeling is for a life of hard work, which caused accidents and often led to quarrels. Bones, seemingly broken deliberately with a fist or stick, were common. One man at Cirencester who sustained sixteen fractured ribs may have been an ill-treated slave.

The excavators of the Trentholme Drive cemetery at York commented soberly that 'there is compelling evidence that the majority of the denizens of second-, third- and fourth-century York could not expect to long survive their fortieth year'. Very few in fact survived the age of forty-five, so that Romano-British 'elderly' is the twentieth-century 'middle-aged'. These figures equal those in any pre-Industrial Revolution society, where, according to Keith Hopkins, life expectancy would be about thirty years. Life in Roman Britain may have been more comfortable for some but it did not imply a long life.

Medical facilities

In theory lives ought to have been longer, for the Romans knew a great deal about medicine and there is evidence for doctors in Britain. Many doctors were Greek and were probably trained using the medical treatises of Galen and Celsus. The majority of their tombstones have been found at the forts, indicating their attachment to the army. The *vicani* may have made use of their services but the general population might be served by a range of practitioners from the highly skilled to mere quacks. In Gaul, doctors were organized into circuits based on guilds situated in market towns; possibly a similar arrangement existed in Britain.

No full set of surgical instruments survives, like those found in the Rhineland at Bingen or in towns in Italy, but a uterine sound has been found at Hockwold (Norfolk), and scalpels, probes, knives and spatulas were discovered on other sites. There is also firm evidence for a trepanning operation being performed on a skull in York.

No doubt good advice by a doctor could have relieved the case of gout found at Cirencester, probably caused by overindulgence in wine and the consumption of an excess of the high purine content of anchovies in garum. Skilful handling would ease the broken bones of the men at Cirencester. Stricter control of temper might have prevented the numerous wounds which the townspeople of York seem to have inflicted on each other. But nothing could cure the cases of leprosy identified in the Poundbury and Cirencester cemeteries, the cases of spinal tuberculosis, and the polio victims at Cirencester and Vindolanda, nor stop the plague which, as Gildas reported, swept through Britain in the fourth century.

Many people would rely on folk remedies. Seeds of henbane, useful as a painkiller, hemlock and poppy found at York may indicate medical usage; plantain can combat dysentery. Plants from Silchester include Good King Henry, self-heal, hemlock, deadly nightshade and St John's Wort. Lumps of realgar have been identified as *auripigmentum,* mentioned by Celsus as an antiseptic to cleanse wounds and ulceration. He also mentions celery as a diuretic, and seeds of wild celery were found in latrine refuse at Bearsden. An amphora, sent to the fort at Carpow, had a Greek word written on it, meaning horehound, a noted remedy for cough complaints; presumably it came ready mixed with wine. Another inscription, *amine,* on an amphora found at Caerleon suggests that the troops were also offered the best Amianean wine from Italy, recommended as a cure for the common cold and for diarrhoea.

Much of the evidence from Britain comes from military sites, where the army would be under constant medical care together with a regime of fitness and exercise. The rest of the inhabitants of Britain would rely on good luck and suitable offerings to the gods of healing to keep them healthy, just as their predecessors had done in Iron Age Britain.

7
Art and decoration

The Celtic inheritance

Appreciation of art is a personal matter, for people's tastes differ. Perhaps in no other area has there been such a reconsideration of standards and style than in that of Romano-British art. In 1926, R. G. Collingwood wrote, 'At its lowest terms the history of Romano-British art can be told in a couple of sentences. Before the Roman conquest the Britons were a race of gifted and brilliant artists: the conquest, forcing them back into their mould of Roman life with its vulgar efficiency and lack of taste, destroyed that gift and reduced art to the level of mere manufacture.' He admitted that the statement was inadequate, but his comments on the 'melancholy story' indicate strong belief. Some artefacts are described as being of a 'blundering stupid ugliness'. Forty years later, Jocelyn Toynbee's comments were more appreciative: 'The works of art that were made in, or imported into [Britain] during a period of 400 years form an impressive part of our national inheritance.'

Collingwood mourned that Rome suppressed a vigorous Celtic abstract art of a highly complex delicacy, which could not come to terms with the figurative representative art of the Romans; Toynbee directed attention to the partnership which existed between Celts and Romans so that the former were able to 'embrace and translate into the native idiom the imperial art and culture of the latter'. One problem is that only a fraction of what was available has survived. Artistic objects having religious connotations were at the mercy of iconoclasts who destroyed them as much for their symbolic role as for their cultural identity.

Yet art represents a meeting of minds. A work of art may be created for its own sake but artists have to survive; the buying power of the client dictates taste. The close relationship of patron and artist is clearly seen in pre-Roman Britain, where late La Tène metalwork satisfied the artistic taste of a warrior aristocracy as well as incorporating decorative and religious motifs, which are subtly understated. Universal Classical motifs – palmette, swastika, circle – merged with Celtic stylization of the human head, birds and animals. The artistic result was an intricate blending so that one glance notes a sinuous form, a second reveals an emerging mask, head or symbol, shape-changing in art as well as literature.

Craftsmen favoured asymmetrical traits, often making use of tendril swirls. Enamelling produced animal faces, especially on shield bosses. In enamel decoration, red was the most constant colour but studs of coral and blue glass were also used. By the first century BC intricately patterned brooches were being created, a tradition which continued in the so-called dragonesque brooches (see **68**) and in the finest shoulder clasp yet found, the Aesica brooch, now in the Museum of Antiquities, Newcastle upon Tyne. Above all, Celtic craftsmen excite admiration for their power of observation. The artists who created the bronze boars discovered at Hounslow (Greater London) and Wattisfield (Suffolk) had

Bronze Boars
Actual size

Wattisfield , Suffolk

Guilden Morden, Cambridgeshire

Colchester, Essex

Hounslow, Middlesex

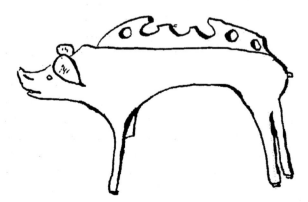

Hounslow, Middlesex

74 Small bronze boars, actual size, display the skill of craftsmen.

noted the beast's paunchy bristling nature (**74**), while the one who wrought the horse found at Silchester had appreciated a powerful striding runner.

Some of the finest artistic examples are the gold collars and torcs, in particular the richly designed ones found in East Anglia. These were probably intended to be worn around the neck, although the weight and awkwardness of some might make for uncomfortable wearing. Some, however, were worn permanently and may designate status. Dio Cassius records that Boudicca 'wore a great gold torc and a multi-coloured tunic folded round her, over which was a thick cloak with a brooch. This was how she always dressed.'

Roman influence

The arrival of the Romans realigned aristocratic patronage. Celtic chieftains, who had adorned themselves with torcs, decorated their horses with reminders of the head cult and used highly decorated weapons, now had to forgo these artefacts. The carrying of weapons in public was forbidden. The subtle transformation of the higher ranks of society into civic leaders meant that other outlets were required for patronage. But a love of jewellery is universal, and women, who had worn jewellery rich both in design and symbolism, were not going to forgo adornment of a more Classical nature.

The art which the Romans brought with them had developed from the Hellenistic culture of the Mediterranean region. It was anthropomorphic, based on the human figure, aiming to create realistic objects not to express abstract symbolism. The human figure was portrayed sometimes with shocking realism, more often in idealized form, as patronage demanded a high standard of expression and finish. This is not to say that there was a uniform style. Motifs and techniques depended upon native craftsmanship throughout the empire so that Roman art might be Greco-Roman art, Near-Eastern Roman art or Romano-British art.

But artists are itinerant. Many were from the Hellenistic parts of the empire and it was they who seem to influence other provincial craftsmen. In Britain they found an aristocratic clientele, who patronized them in order to indicate their loyalty to Roman ways.

Throughout the empire a huge trade in works of art resulted in artefacts becoming models setting standards of taste. Some objects had already reached Britain in the first century BC. Rich cremation burials at Welwyn reveal a mixture of tastes – Celtic fire-dogs with stylized ox-heads, human masks, which may have decorated cups, and silver cups of Classical design. In the aristocratic Lexden grave was a medallion of Augustus, handsome furniture-fittings and fragments of gold fabric. A head of a griffin might have been appreciated for its mythological attributes but the bronze figures of a boar and a bull seem to have been imported from Gaul.

Mosaics

After AD 43 new techniques were demanded from British craftsmen, which perhaps they were unable or unwilling to fulfil. Mosaic-working is a case in point. A man with a little technical dexterity and ability to follow repetitive pattern could earn a living, but the trade also required a skill passed on from the master mosaicist to the pupil. Designs were possibly copied from pattern books which were compiled using inspiration from Hellenistic sources. Mosaic-workers soon found their way to Britain. Mosaics in the bath-house of the legionary fortress at Exeter, dated to AD 55–60, indicate that officials and administrators demanded the same level of comfort as they had experienced on their last posting.

Several reasons might be suggested for commissioning mosaics in Britain. On artistic grounds, for example; geometrical designs, such as the one found in a second-century house at Aldborough, would be attractive to families who had enjoyed the abstract patterning of Celtic art (**colour plate 12**). But pavements had a utilitarian function, too, providing an easily cleaned, bright floor covering, although as mosaics were

costly and immovable, their subject-matter required some thought before they were commissioned. Hence the value of the pattern book. To replace a mosaic meant laying one on top of another as happened at Fishbourne, where the new owner may have been tempted to order a scene in a pattern book depicting sea-panthers and showing an admirable roundel of a boy on a dolphin. Mosaics may subtly indicate solidarity with the new regime or provide an indication of the patron's status.

Patrons in south-west Britain might commission mosaics from workshops centred on

75 *The central panel of the mosaic in the Lullingstone villa, Kent. Bellerophon riding Pegasus is killing the Chimaera, a monster with a goat's head, a lion's body and a dragon's tail, surrounded by playful dolphins. In the corners are three surviving heads representing the seasons. A swallow sits on the shoulder of Spring, Autumn wears a garland of corn in the hair and Winter wears a* cucullus.

Cirencester and Dorchester, which specialized in the design of Orpheus charming prowling animals. The magnificent one at Woodchester (Glos.), 14sq m (150sq ft), is the largest known north of the Alps. Sometimes an owner wanted something outstanding. At Bignor, mosaics revealing cupids acting as gladiators and a head of Venus, whose nimbus glitters with green glass tesserae, were created by a master craftsman who signed his work with the abbreviation *TER*. Mosaic-workers used various materials to create their designs: Purbeck marble for black and blue, chalk and limestone for cream, white and pink, sandstones and tiles for red and brown. Tiles were fired to give shades of grey and pink. Red glass creates vivid blood on the wounded Actaeon's thigh at Cirencester. Heaps of tesserae, sorted into piles by colour, at the Rudston and Gadebridge (Herts.) villas, seem to have been left by the mosaicist in case running repairs were necessary.

Looking at some of the mosaics raises certain questions. Mythological scenes were extremely popular, not only familiar ones portraying Bacchus, Venus and Neptune, but more obscure stories of Lysurgus and the nymph Ambrosia, and Ceres and Triptolemus. Did the villa owners at Lullingstone and Keynsham appreciate the story of Bellerophon and the Chimaera (**75**) or did the picture attract them? How familiar was the owner of the Low Ham villa in Dorset with the story of Dido and Aeneas (see **colour plate 3**)? Did he show the mosaicist a picture from an illustrated manuscript or did the mosaicist produce one from his pattern book? Jocelyn Toynbee suggests the design may have come from North Africa.

Did the citizen of Aldborough mind that the mosaicist lacked the skill to make the wolf and the twins realistic (**76**)? Were there two mosaic-workers at Rudston, one competent in the Classical tradition so that the portrayal of the charioteer conveys the vigour of the race, and another worker intent on producing a Celtic female fertility figure? Or did the patron demand mosaics which indicated his Classical tendencies while still placating Celtic deities (**77**)? Did the masters of the Corinium school based around Cirencester undertake complicated work of designing figures and animals but leave the apprentices to lay out the more repetitive parts of the design?

Wall paintings

Wall paintings also reveal convergence of taste. Many were of Classical design, understandable as their interpreters were used to working in the Classical medium of fresco where the surface was carefully prepared for durability by the plasterer with coats of lime and gypsum (**colour plate 13**). If one layer dried out, it had to be keyed before the next could be applied, as a plasterer at Leicester had to do. Vitruvius had recommended at least six layers of plaster but in Britain the average appears to be two.

Pigments were made from a variety of sources: black from charcoal or lampblack, white from white lime, to mix with other colours for subtle shades. Red, composed of oxides of iron, and brown from sinapis, a similar ochre, were used

76 *The craftsman, who created the wolf feeding the twins Romulus and Remus on a mosaic at a house in Aldborough, North Yorkshire, had problems with the perspective of both the animal and the twins, but the villa owner may have been content with the portrayal, as if the meaning of the design rather than the artistic concept was important.*

77 *The Venus pavement from the Rudston villa, North Yorkshire. The geometric design shows the hand of a master craftsman, while the figure of Venus is lacking in proportion. This is possibly because it is representing a Celtic fertility goddess.*

extensively on the walls of some houses in Verulamium. Vermilion was produced from mineral cinnabar by heating and washing the ore to remove impurities. The woad plant provided blue, so did basic copper carbonate and imported lapis lazuli. Blue frit, artificially prepared from copper silicate and calcium by firing in crucibles, was found at Woodeaton (Oxon.), as if ready to be sold. Purple, made from a Tyrian species of sea mollusc, was expensive. Vitruvius suggests

using the juice of whortleberries (bilberries) mixed in milk; these would be easy to obtain in Britain. A little gold leaf has been found at Lincoln, London and Colchester, where wealthy patrons would appreciate the value of such work.

Some scenes recall Celtic decoration: a patterned ceiling at Verulamium invokes a recollection of enamel studs, and birds and animals reminiscent of those once displayed in metal, while the wall panels resemble marbled alabaster separated by columns. At Kingscote (Glos.), in the late third century, painter and patron had chosen a painting which represents the story of Achilles' love for Deidameia, daughter of the King of Skyros. The hero is seated, shield by his side, with Cupid hovering in the background. One house at

Catterick had a room repainted three times, not perhaps an unusual occurrence if the occupants became bored or irritated by a design; new owners would also wish to impose their own tastes.

Sculpture

Abstract patterning and naturalistic scenes presented few problems to craftsmen imbued with the Celtic tradition; portrayals of human figures caused difficulties, which is obvious in a study of the tombstones. Some, however, were created by competent craftsmen skilled in sculpture. The tombstone of the centurion Marcus Favonius Facilis, at Colchester, would stand comparison with any made in Rome. Others show a hankering after the abstract concept. On the tombstone of Marcus Aurelius Nepos and his wife at Chester, the centurion's uniform is merely a hint of what might have been, while his wife's garment lovingly depicts linear patterning.

Juvenius, the carver of the figures of Romulus and the *Genius* found at Custom Scrubs, Bisley, had some problems with their forms of dress, but Gulioepius, who commissioned the *Genius,* was obviously satisfied with the result. Close by, at Bath, were Priscus and Sulinus, the first from the tribe of the Carnutes in Gaul, the other working locally, for he dedicated another altar at Gloucester. Priscus describes himself as a stonemason (*lapidarius*), Sulinus as a *sculptor.*

Imported works of art could provide models for British craftsmen. A native artist might have seen the statue of the river god imported into London, noted the angle of the head and attempted to produce a similar statue at Cirencester; only the heads of both these reclining forms survive. The reclining river god at Chesters, who presided over the waters of the North Tyne, copies the artistic style of the Classical deity (**78**). In the second century, visitors to the Lullingstone villa could have admired the portrait busts of the owners, while privately considering how they could arrange to be

78 *A statue of a bearded river god, probably representing the River Tyne, found at Chesters on Hadrian's Wall. The pose recalls that created by more Classically trained sculptors to portray river deities such as the Tiber.*

similarly immortalized. The stone female head, crowned with layers of tight curls, found at Bath, could indicate that its owner had insisted upon having a hairstyle in the very latest first-century fashion.

Smaller works

Works of art such as mosaics, wall paintings and even tombstones, are ordered with a particular purpose in mind, most likely as a one-off purchase. Smaller objects are bought because the buyers like them or want to present them as a gift. Pre-Roman Britain had no use for seal-boxes and gemstones; for the Romans they were a necessity. Classical designs, carved on precious stones and set into rings to act as a seal device, were routine practice and the purchase of these designs – deities, animals or abstract concepts – was a matter of personal and significant choice.

79 Amulets, especially those bearing a Medusa head, believed to ward off evil were very popular. This one sketched on a bone disc was found in the Lullingstone mausoleum.

Many were imported, but Martin Henig has identified a workshop at Carlisle, which worked in red jasper and cornelian. Another workshop may have been at Snettisham, where a jeweller's hoard contained 110 cornelian gemstones, many with crudely carved but recognizable Roman deities.

Gemstones are both practical and luxurious objects, as also is jewellery. A thriving industry in jet, established in the Whitby region, exported its products to the Rhineland. Small figures of bears, found at Malton and Colchester, reveal careful observation of the characteristics of this animal. Most popular were the round medallion portraits, some bearing Medusa's head to ward off evil (**79**). Other forms of amulets, created in bronze, were in the shape of a wheel or the phallus. Brooches and bracelets, required as accessories, continued in ornamentation the Celtic tradition. Dragonesque and trumpet-scrolled brooches, usually made of bronze, often enamelled and occasionally tinned to represent silver, use hatching and the flowing lines of animal forms. By the second century, trumpet, disc and fantail brooches seem to be the most popular forms. Later these are replaced by the cross-bow type.

Jewellery is a minor art form where fashion dominates according to personal choice. Table settings display an art form and the personal work of the designer. Imported luxury goods, status symbols of conspicuous consumption, include displays of silver plate like that found at Mildenhall (see **58**). The huge intricately decorated silver dish has a maritime theme in its centre where nereids and marine animals surround the head of Oceanus. Round these dance maenads in Bacchic revel. A proud host would have drawn a guest's attention to such a treasure. Such works were equally attractive to thieves. The hoards of late Roman silver found at Traprain Law (East Lothian) and Coleraine (County Derry, Northern Ireland) were probably looted from wealthy Romano-British households.

Much of the glass would be domestic ware, some of it made in the workshops of Caister by Norwich, Norfolk, and Wilderspool in Cheshire, where fine silica sand is found. But prized

possessions came from the Rhineland where the Cologne and Trier workshops produced so-called snake-thread vessels, examples of which have been found at London and Canterbury. Some glass was wheel-cut; a handsome facet-cut vase survived at Banwell (Avon). A fourth-century engraved glass vessel showing a hare-hunt was found at Wint Hill (Som.) and another with dancing satyrs and maenads came from Dorchester. Prized pieces were put into graves to give pleasure to their owners in the next world.

Craftsmen and patrons

Bronze figurines imported into Britain as part of the tradition of objects displayed on *lararia* (see **21** and **80**) provided models for British craftsmen. Many crude figurines of Minerva (**80**) and Mercury (see **15**) are attempts to copy more handsome figures like those found at Plaxtol and Colchester. Similarity of figurines of Hercules found in the Suffolk area (see **14**) suggest the presence of a workshop there and one was certainly situated at Gestingthorpe in Essex, where a clay matrix of Mars was found.

An inscription on one bronze from the Foss Dyke gives some details (**81**). The artist, Celatus, made a figure of Mars for two brothers, Bruccius and Caratius, who had Latinized their surname to Colasunius. They wished their generosity to be recognized, for the inscription continued that they had paid 100 sesterces from their own purse; Celatus, not to be outdone, added that he had given a pound of bronze prepared for the casting. The large figurine displays great competence, even though the measurements of the limbs would have been regarded as being slightly out of proportion by a craftsman trained entirely in the Classical tradition. Celatus, who describes himself as a bronzeworker, may have been an itinerant craftsman visiting Britain or a Celtic artist with a Latinized name, who had learned his skill from a Classically trained master.

A survey of the large number of works of art found in Britain can often distinguish between imported works of art, which reveal a Classical heritage, and those, either imported or carved in

80 *Two bronze figurines of Minerva, one from Lincoln, height 10.6cm (4.2in), the other from Plaxtol, Kent, height 18cm (7.1in), showing differing qualities of workmanship.*

Britain, which are dependent upon Celtic tradition, many being the work of itinerant Celticized artists who came to Britain seeking patrons. Some of these patrons probably altered radically their concept of art during the early years of the conquest, which forced artists to undergo a similar readjustment of ideas. This, in turn, meant a change of technique, which could not always be accomplished.

Objects, however, are not necessarily bought for their aesthetic value. A crudely made one may have given enormous pleasure to its buyer because it had social cachet or be a reminder of an event. Crude bronze figurines of deities displayed on a *lararium* are a public affirmation that their owner worshipped Roman not Celtic deities. But that person might buy a statue of a Celtic deity to place in a woodland grove, thus concealing another side to his personality.

Public expression of artistic form was made at an official level. Statues were paid for by individuals or by corporate patrons. The heads of the Emperors Claudius (see **2**) and Hadrian, found discarded as loot, came from official statues set up respectively in Colchester and London. Craftsmen, commissioned to decorate temples,

81 *The bronze figurine of Mars, height 25.5cm (10in), found at the Foss Dyke, Lincolnshire.*

palaces, basilicas and official residences, would seek commissions elsewhere. Classically trained craftsmen passed on their skills to men who had decided that to obtain work they must change their style. Tom Blagg, in a study of column bases and capitals, has deduced the presence of 'schools' of stonemasons in Britain, that is, men who executed common styles and methods of execution and were employed by civilian and military authorities. These schools had long lives and were wide ranging, one spreading from Cirencester, Silchester and Caerwent in the late first and second centuries, another seemingly connecting Cirencester, Verulamium, Lincoln and Canterbury in the second and third centuries.

Itinerant craftsmen, like the medieval masons, travelled far in their search for work, changing style and technique to suit their patrons. Continuity of abstract expression and love of decoration derived from naturalistic patterns emerge in a variety of forms. Official art, following the Classical tradition, was intended to act as a model but Celticized tradition never completely disappeared. It did not 'go underground' as Collingwood implied, but retained a considerable hold on Romano-British taste. In the post-Roman period Celtic art reasserted itself, especially when it found a new patron in the Christian Church.

Conclusion

The conclusion to one of A.E. Housman's poems in *A Shropshire Lad* expresses the passage of time:

> Today the Roman and his trouble
> Are ashes under Uricon.

Yet this is not the experience of the British reader. Roman Britain is one of the most popular periods of history possibly because some of the activities of the Romans have a fascination beyond what they deserve – gladiatorial contests in the amphitheatre, glorified triumphs and gluttonous banquets attract disproportionate attention. Other areas, such as military discipline and competent civilian administration, arouse sympathetic recognition. The expansion of the Roman empire and its subsequent decline have been compared to the expansion and contraction of the British empire. The features which gaze from Roman portrait busts are those of Victorian colonial administrators or are paralleled in our own newspapers.

In Britain archaeological excavations continue to interest the general public. The queues to view the newly discovered Temple of Mithras in the City of London in 1954 were long and continuous, comparable to the successive groups of people watching the uncovering of part of the London forum in the 1980s. Although a great deal is known about the artefacts and buildings of Roman Britain, there is still much to be learned. More detailed examination of organic material has revealed what was eaten and drunk but the quantity of food consumed and the cooking methods used are lacking. Did Romano-British women know and use Apicius' cookery book or were cooking methods passed on from mother to daughter, much as happens today? Possibly expectations are too great. Bath systems and hypocausts found in Britain give rise to the belief that all Romano-British people had the advantages of central heating and hot baths.

The Romano-British period lasted only slightly less in time than that which has passed from the beginning of the Tudor period to the present day. Over that period life-styles have altered enormously. This was probably the case in Roman Britain, which because of its easily classified definition is considered as a continuous whole. Attempts can be made to define the life-styles of people in the towns as opposed to those in the country. It is perhaps reasonably easy to outline the sequential development of single sites. It is less easy to note changes in habitat and thought. Models may be produced to suggest why people act in certain ways, although any particular action can be negated by the element of chance. Human beings are often unpredictable in their actions. Yet the same passions of love, hatred, compassion and envy are present in every era. By examining objects and deducing how they were used, by making comparisons with other societies and trying to understand how people acted within their own society, and underpinning research with academic discipline, a re-creation of a past era can emerge.

Glossary

balsamarium A small container for incense or perfume often made in the form of a grotesque figure.

beneficarii Soldiers detached from a legion for a specific period or for specific duties.

biga A two-horse chariot.

byrrus Britannicus A long cloak of heavy wool, which was exported from Britain.

chi-rho The first two letters of Christ's name in Greek, used as a monogram.

civitas A tribal community which would be under the administration of the main town, the *civitas*-capital.

cochleare Small spoon used for eating eggs and prising molluscs and shellfish from their shells.

colonia A town with a special status, where the inhabitants were Roman citizens, usually established to house retired veteran soldiers. The title could also be granted to a town as an honour.

comes Title granted to the commander of a field army in the fourth century AD.

cucullus A hooded cloak.

dux Title granted to the commander of frontier forces in the fourth century AD.

equites The order of knights, second in the social scale beneath the senators.

forum The central market square or open space. One side usually had the basilica or main hall, the other could have other important buildings such as temples.

haruspex A religious official attached to a temple who studied the entrails of sacrificed animals.

lararium (Plural *lararia*) A household shrine taking the form of a raised platform or a shelf.

lares Bronze figurines of household gods, found in pairs, and representing two young men, each poised on one foot, wearing high boots and a short flared tunic, and holding up drinking horns.

mansio A guest-house used by official travellers.

mirmillones Gladiators who had a short sword and an oblong shield, and wore a heavy helmet decorated with a fish.

mortaria Rough pottery with a pouring lip and with grit baked into the bottom on which food could be pulverized.

municipia Towns having Latin status, where the people could have the status of Roman citizens.

olla A wide-mouthed vessel in which food could be cooked.

ordo A town council composed of 100 members, elected by a property qualification.

patellae Round shallow pans.

paterae Hemispherical-shaped pans.

patinae Deep pans.

Pax Romana Phrase used to indicate the pacification which the Romans established over the empire.

penates The spirits of the household store cupboard, who were worshipped in order to promote the prosperity of the household. They were invoked before starting or ending a journey.

peregrini Non-Roman citizens living in the provinces.

polae Small mortars for pounding herbs.

quadriga A four-horse chariot.

retiarius A gladiator who fought with a net and a trident and protected one arm with a raised guard of leather and metal.

sacerdos A priest, usually attached to a Classical-style temple.

seviri Augustales Wealthy merchant freedmen organized into colleges of six, who acted as priests of the imperial cult and sacrificed to the emperor's numen.

stola A sleeveless or short-sleeved tunic.

tauroctony A portrayal of Mithras killing the wild bull, usually placed at the end of the Mithraeum.

tesserae Small stones set into a mosaic floor to make up the pattern.

vicus (Plural *vici*) A small settlement. The term usually refers to a civilian settlement outside a fort.

villa A Latin word for a house or a farm usually connected with farming, which often depended on a town for its economy.

Places to visit

There are many visible remains of the Roman presence in Britain both on the ground or in museums. The places mentioned below are only a few which can be visited but they refer to the most significant examples mentioned in the text.

Aldborough, North Yorkshire
North-west of York, reached by A59 and B6265. The town walls and two mosaics are to be seen. The mosaic of the wolf and the twins is in the Leeds City Museum. (English Heritage)

Bath, Avon
The Roman remains, beneath the Georgian Pump Room, include the hot spring, the Great Bath and a suite of baths. Finds include altars, gemstones, curse tablets, the gorgon's head from the pediment of the Temple of Sul Minerva and the bronze head of the cult statue of Minerva.

Bignor, West Sussex
Reached by a side road from A29 at the village of Bury. A fine group of mosaics includes geometric patterns, the panel of cupids acting the role of gladiators and the head of Venus.

Caerleon, Gwent
Outside the remains of the fort lies the amphitheatre. The recently excavated baths are now on view. (Cadw: Welsh Historic Monuments)

Chedworth, Gloucestershire
Near Yanworth and reached by a road from A429. The villa remains include bath suites and mosaics, including the personification of Winter wearing a *cucullus*. (National Trust)

Chesterholm (Vindolanda)
Reached from a minor road, running north from Bardon Mill on the A69. An extensive excavation programme has revealed the remains of the fort and the civil settlement. (English Heritage)

Cirencester, Gloucestershire
The amphitheatre lies to the south-west of the town. (English Heritage) By the river are the remains of the defences. The museum contains mosaic pavements of the Corinium school and a reconstructed Roman living-room. Finds from the excavations include the Christian chi-rho acrostic, reliefs and statuary.

Colchester, Essex
The walls of the *colonia* are still visible. (English Heritage) The excellent museum, containing a collection of Roman objects, is in the Norman castle, which was built on the vaults of the temple of Claudius.

Fishbourne, West Sussex
About 2.5km (1½miles) west of Chichester, signposted from A27 at Fishbourne village. The remains of the large villa or palace have been preserved under cover. The main reason for visiting is to see the mosaics and the restored garden.

Great Witcombe, Gloucestershire
Signposted from A417 leading east from Gloucester. The extensive remains indicate how the winged-corridor villa was laid out on a terraced south-facing slope. (English Heritage)

Leicester, Leicestershire
By the side of the museum lie the remains of the great baths of which a wall survives. (English Heritage)

London
There are rooms devoted to excavated finds from Roman Britain in the British Museum and the Museum of London. It is still possible to made a circuit of the layout of the defensive wall.

Lullingstone, Kent
Signposted from Eynsford on A225, just south of A20. The remains of the villa and the mosaics are preserved under cover. Several finds, including the wall paintings, are in the British Museum. (English Heritage)

Lydney Park, Gloucestershire
Reached from A48 between Gloucester and Chepstow. The remains of the temple of Nodens and the adjoining buildings can be seen. As the site is privately owned, permission for a visit has to be obtained from the Lydney Park Estate Office (Tel 01594 42844).

Maiden Castle, Dorset
Signposted from A354, south of Dorchester. The outline foundations of the Roman temple are visible in the centre of the hill-fort. From here there is a splendid view looking towards Dorchester, the Roman town founded when the inhabitants were removed from the hill-fort. (English Heritage)

North Leigh, Oxfordshire
Signposted from A4095, north-east of Witney. Two wings are visible of the extensive courtyard villa. There is a fine mosaic with a geometric pattern. (English Heritage)

St Albans, Hertfordshire
The exposed Roman remains of Verulamium include the theatre, foundations of houses and the defences. (English Heritage) The refurbished museum gives an excellent introduction to civilian life in Roman Britain.

Silchester, Hampshire
About 13km (8 miles) south of Reading. There are extensive remains of the defences and the recently excavated amphitheatre. (English Heritage) The finds are in the Reading Museum.

South Shields, Tyne and Wear
The remains of the granaries of the Roman fort indicate the large corn supply grown in Britain. The museum contains the tombstone of Regina.

Wall, Staffordshire
About 3km (2 miles) south-west of Lichfield. The remains of the bath-house and the *mansio* are visible. (English Heritage/National Trust)

Wroxeter, Shropshire
About 8km (5 miles) east of Shrewsbury on B4380. The south wall of the exercise hall and the remains of the baths are displayed. (English Heritage) The finds are in the site museum and in Rowley's House Museum in Shrewsbury.

Further reading

General reading

A good short history is Malcolm Todd *Roman Britain (55 BC–AD 400)* (1981). More detailed are S.S. Frere *Britannia: a history of Roman Britain* (3rd edn, 1987) and Peter Salway *Roman Britain* (1981). Salway's book has also been issued as *The Oxford Illustrated History of Roman Britain* (1992). Other general histories are J.S. Wacher *Roman Britain* (1978), M. Millett *Roman Britain* (1995) and T.W. Potter and Catherine Johns *Roman Britain* (1992), which has a useful bibliography. R.G. Collingwood and J.N.L. Myers *Roman Britain and the English Settlements* (1937) still has some value. Peter Clayton has edited a series of essays in *Companion to Roman Britain* (1980). Joan Liversidge's *Britain in the Roman Empire* (1968) looked beyond the province. R.J.A. Wilson *A Guide to the Roman Remains in Britain* (1988) is invaluable for visiting sites.

A collection of source material is S. Ireland *Roman Britain: a sourcebook* (1986). Caesar's *Gallic Wars*, Tacitus *Agricola* and *The Annals of Imperial Rome*, and Suetonius *Lives of the Twelve Caesars* are available in Penguin Classics.

Society and administration

A detailed introduction to the people of Roman Britain based mainly on the epigraphic evidence is to be found in Anthony Birley's *The People of Roman Britain* (1979) and *The Fasti of Roman Britain* (1981). The question of Romanization in Britain was considered by Francis Haverfield *The Romanisation of Roman Britain* (2nd edn, 1923). Other discussions are in Martin Millett *Romanisation of Britain* (1990) and Richard Hingley *Rural Settlement in Britain* (1989). For general discussion see Richard Reece 'Romanisation: a point of view' in T.F.C. Blagg and M. Millett (eds) *The Early Roman Empire in the West* (1990).

The question of education is touched on in A. Burnett 'Knowledge of Literary Classics in Roman Britain', *Britannia* 9 (1978), 307–13. Slavery as part of the economy is covered in M.I. Finley *The Ancient Economy* (2nd edn, 1985) and politically in F. Miller 'Condemnation to Hard Labour in the Roman Empire, from the Julio-Claudians to Constantine', *Papers of the British School at Rome* 52 (1984), 124–47. A detailed study of slave chains in Western Europe is given in Hugh Thompson 'Iron Age and Roman Slave-Shackles', *Archaeological Journal* 150 (1993), 57–168.

Religion, belief and death

For Celtic religion see Graham Webster *The British Celts and their Gods under Rome* (1986); Martin Henig covers a broader area in *Religion in Roman Britain* (1984). Essays on individual deities are detailed in Martin Henig and Anthony King (eds) *Pagan Gods and Shrines of the Roman Empire* (1986). For Christianity see A.C. Thomas *Christianity in Roman Britain to AD 500* (1981) and D. Watts *Christians and Pagans in the Roman Empire* (1991). Bath is covered by Barry Cunliffe in *Roman Bath Discovered* (1984) and *Roman Bath* (1995). Roger Tomlin has a section on the curse tablets in Volume II of the Oxford University Committee for Archaeology Monograph No. 16 on *The Roman Temple of Sulis Minerva*. A. Woodward's *Shrines and Sacrifice* (1992) discusses temples and shrines.

General surveys of burial rites can be found in J.M.C. Toynbee *Death and Burial in the Roman World* (1971), Richard Reece (ed.) *Burial in the Roman World,* Council for British Archaeology Research Report No. 22 (1977) and S. Walker *Memorials to the Roman Dead* (1985). The Royal Commission on Historical Monuments has published detailed volumes on *Eboracum: Roman York* (1962) and *Roman London* (1928) which contain catalogues of graves and types of burial. Giles Clarke *The Roman Cemetery at Lankhills,* Winchester Studies 3 (1979), gives details of the Winchester burials and L.P. Wenham excavated *The Romano-British Cemetery at Trentholme Drive, York* (1968).

Recreation and leisure

Descriptions of urban public buildings can be found in J.S. Wacher *Towns of Roman Britain* (1990). A detailed monograph of the amphitheatre at Silchester has been published by the Society for Roman Studies *Britannia* Monograph No. 10 (1989). Michael Grant's *Gladiators* (1967) records the profession of these men. Tony Rook has produced an interesting account of *Roman Baths in Britain,* Shire Archaeology (1992).

Housing and domestic life

Plans of houses and details of town life can be found in J.S. Wacher *Towns of Roman Britain* (1995) and Guy de la Bédoyère *Roman Towns in Britain* (1992). The same author has also written *Roman Villas and the Countryside* (1993) which contains house-plans and reconstructions. Other surveys of villas in Britain are A.L.F. Rivet (ed.) *The Roman Villa in Britain* (1969), D.E. Johnston *Roman Villas,* Shire Archaeology (1988) and M. Todd *Studies in the Romano-British Villa* (1978). This contains a paper by J.T. Smith on villas as a key to the social structure. G.W. Meates published the Lullingstone villa in detail in two volumes (1979, 1987). Alec McWhirr has provided evidence for housing in Cirencester and Gloucester in *Roman Gloucestershire* (1981) and *Houses in Roman Cirencester* (1986). Also useful is G.C. Boon *Silchester: the Roman town of Calleva* (1974) and G. Milne *Roman London* (1995).

Food and drink

There are several translations of Apicius. The most accurate is *Apicius, De Re Coquinaria* edited by Barbara Flower and Elizabeth Rosenbaum as *The Roman Cookery Book* (1958). A later one is *Apicius, Cooking and Dining in Ancient Rome* translated by Joseph Vehling (1977). V. Swan *Pottery in Roman Britain,* Shire Archaeology (4th edn, 1988) is a concise summary. The extensive range of Roman glassware is covered in D.B. Harden *Glass of the Caesars* (1987).

Clothing and hygiene

Women's clothing is touched on in L. Allison-Jones *Women in Roman Britain.* John Peter Wild covers textiles in 'Clothing in the North-West Provinces of the Roman Empire', *Sonderdruck aus Bonner Jahrbuch* 168 (1968), 166–240, *Textile Manufacture in the Northern Roman Provinces* (1979) and *Textiles in Archaeology,* Shire Archaeology (1988). Lily M. Wilson dealt exhaustively with clothing in *The Roman Toga* (1924) and *The Clothing of the Ancient Romans* (1938).

Ralph Jackson's wide-ranging study of *Doctors and Diseases in the Roman Empire* (1988) contains details of hygiene and medicine. Several reports on the cemeteries contain evidence of the injuries to bodies such as A. McWhirr, L. Viner and C. Wells *Romano-British Cemeteries at Cirencester* (1982).

Art

Two studies of Celtic Art are I.M. Stead *Celtic Art* (1985) and R. Megaw and V. Megaw *Early Celtic Art in Britain and Ireland* (1986). The Roman area is covered by Martin Henig in *The Art of Roman Britain* (1995), Martin Henig (ed.) *A Handbook of Roman Art* (1983) and D. Strong and D. Brown *Roman Crafts* (1976). A smaller study is A. McWhirr *Roman Crafts and Industries,* Shire Archaeology (1982). J.M.C. Toynbee's two studies *Art in Roman Britain* (1962) and *Art in Britain under the Romans* (1964) are invaluable. Studies of mosaics include A. Rainey *Mosaics in Roman Britain* (1973) and D.S. Neal *Mosaics in Roman Britain* (1981). Other books on decoration include N. Davey and R. Ling *Wall-Painting in Roman Britain* (1982) and R. Ling *Romano-British Wall-Painting,* Shire Archaeology (1985).

Index

The Author

Joan Alcock took a first degree in history and then further degrees in archaeology at the Institute of Archaeology, University of London. She lectures and writes on history, archaeology and environmental subjects and specializes in the history of food as part of her academic work at South Bank University, London. In connection with her research she has travelled widely in Europe and the Far East.

This volume is part of a major series, jointly conceived for English Heritage and Batsford.

Titles in the series:

Places of Interest
Avebury Caroline Malone
Dartmoor Sandy Gerrard
Hadrian's Wall Stephen Johnson
St Augustine's Abbey, Canterbury Richard Gemetal
Stonehenge Julian Richards
Winchester Tom Beaumont Jones

Periods
Anglo-Saxon England Martin Welch
Bronze Age Britain Michael Parker Pearson
Industrial England Michael Stratton and Barrie Trinder
Iron Age Britain Barry Cunliffe
Norman England Trevor Rowley
Roman Britain Martin Millett
Stone Age Britain Nicholas Barton
Viking Age England Julian D. Richards

Subjects
Castles Tom McNeill
Channel Defences Andrew Saunders
Cistercian Abbeys of Britain David Robinson (ed.)
Life in Roman Britain Joan Alcock
Ships and Shipwrecks Peter Marsden

'**One of the great classic series of British archaeology.**' *Current Archaeology*

128